Sand and Fire

SAND
AND
FIRE

EXPLORING A RARE
PINE BARRENS LANDSCAPE

DAVE PETERS

WISCONSIN HISTORICAL SOCIETY PRESS

Published by the Wisconsin Historical Society Press
Publishers since 1855

The Wisconsin Historical Society helps people connect to the past by collecting,
preserving, and sharing stories. Founded in 1846, the Society is one of the nation's
finest historical institutions.
Join the Wisconsin Historical Society: wisconsinhistory.org/membership

Publication of this book was made possible in part by a gift from
Furthermore: a program of the J. M. Kaplan Fund.
Additional funding was provided by a grant from the Amy Louise
Hunter fellowship fund.

Photos by Dave Peters unless otherwise credited. Front cover photograph: north unit
of the Namekagon Barrens Wildlife Area, by Don McConkey. Frontispiece: south unit
bog in Autumn, by Dave Peters.
Printed in Canada
Typesetting by Integrated Composition Systems

27   26   25   24   23   1   2   3   4   5

Library of Congress Cataloging-in-Publication Data

Names: Peters, Dave, 1952–   author.
Title: Sand and fire: exploring a rare pine barrens landscape/Dave Peters.
Description: [Madison] : Wisconsin Historical Society Press, [2023] |
    Includes bibliographical references and index.
Identifiers: LCCN 2022040081 (print) | LCCN 2022040082 (e-book) |
    ISBN 9781976600050 (paperback) | ISBN 9781976600067 (e-pub)
Subjects: LCSH : Namekagon Barrens Wildlife Area (Wis.)—History. |
    Pine barrens—Wisconsin—History.
Classification: LCC F587.N36 P48 2023 (print) | LCC F587.N36 (e-book) |
    DDC 977.5/1—dc23/eng/20221019
LC record available at https://lccn.loc.gov/2022040081
LC e-book record available at https://lccn.loc.gov/2022040082

For Lisa

"Something of our relationship to the earth is determined
by the particular place we stand at a given time. If you stand
still long enough to observe carefully the things around you,
you will find beauty, and you will know wonder."

N. Scott Momaday,
Earth Keeper: Reflections on the American Land

CONTENTS

The foundation of the Forest Home School, which closed its doors more than eighty years ago, lies almost hidden in this view looking to the northwest.

1

Coming Upon the Barrens

On a mild, sun-filled July morning, I was picking blueberries about a quarter mile south of the pristine Namekagon River in northwestern Wisconsin. The sky was a fresh blue, a promise of afternoon heat kissed the air, and I was daydreaming about the Christmas blueberry cobbler that has become a tradition in my family. Not far away in the brush was a family from nearby Spooner, also picking berries and chatting.

Suddenly one of the women stood up from her children and her ice cream bucket of berries, looked around the clearing, and asked with some awe in her voice, "Where *are* we?"

"The barrens!" I hollered, trying to be helpful.

"How do you spell that?" she wondered.

This book is my answer to both of her questions. She is among the many people, near and far, who have been intrigued by this unusual landscape with a rich human history but know little about it.

Let's start in the middle of the Namekagon Barrens Wildlife Area. We're just beside a sandy road named St. Croix Trail. About five miles to the southwest, the tannin-laced, sturgeon-filled Namekagon River flows into the St. Croix River. Every summer, thousands of canoeists, fishermen, and tubers float past that wooded river junction. But not many folks stop here.

A dark concrete foundation about thirty-six by thirty feet lies in the brush. Three jack pines lean over what was once the tiny Forest Home

School. For several decades in the early 1900s, children walked, rode horses, or sleighed here to receive an education. A succession of women taught at the school over the years. The building burned once, was rebuilt by nearby residents, and finally closed in 1938. What little remains is nearly hidden, and bluebirds and swallows vie to use the wooden box behind the foundation for nesting.

Mark this point on your mental map. It may not look like it, but a lot has happened here. Roaring meltwaters once poured from thick glaciers, leaving deep deposits of sand. People known today as Paleo-Indians likely hunted here with stone-tipped spears. Later came people tracking deer and picking berries. Fire after fire burned. Treaties forced the land to change hands. Surveyors, loggers, and land speculators came and went. Stagecoaches rolled through. Probably a dozen languages were spoken within earshot at one point. Farmers tried to work the land and then left. Habitat conservationists squabbled with foresters.

But for now, if you have come upon these barrens for the first time, just notice the expanse. A land you thought was supposed to wrap you in the blanket of a dark northern forest is missing its trees and instead leaves you bathed in light. It delivers nothing so much as a sense of space.

A pasqueflower pokes its head up in May.

You perhaps have been driving shadowed roads amid plantations of tall red pines and impenetrable thickets of jack pines. Maybe you've been canoeing and fishing the shady Namekagon or St. Croix, paddling waters that in legendary logging days were clogged with felled white pines.

The nearest towns are Minong, fifteen miles east, and Danbury, twenty miles southwest, both catering to the owners of lake country cabins and resorts.

You've been thinking woods.

But here on the barrens, spread over about ten square miles on either side of the Namekagon River, the world opens and light floods the land. Sparse jack pines and stubby oak trees four or five feet high dominate the landscape under a big dome of sky. Solitary red pines stand as sentinels here and there, but you can see the horizon all around. Grasses, sedges, brush, and wildflowers stretch out and invite you to walk.

This is not the North Woods most of us have come to expect in this part of the world. But you can make a pretty strong case that this is the way it should be.

I feel a pull to get out on the land every time I visit the barrens. Maybe it's my prairie upbringing. Maybe it's an appreciation that the network of plants here is constantly in flux, as well as rare. Maybe it's knowing that, for all the land's emptiness, many people have preceded me and tried to thrive here.

I think the same thought every time: put one foot in front of the other, tread the sandy ground, and observe. What I see is different each time.

On an early spring day, delicate pastel pasqueflowers emerge from the dry sand next to the old school foundation. Wild? Or planted a hundred years ago by a young teacher or student?

Blueberries thrive in the sand of the barrens.
PHOTO BY EMILY PETERS

A crescent moon rises on the north unit as the dawn silhouettes an old oak.

In July, the sharp tang of blueberries is a reminder that people have enjoyed the bounty here for thousands of years.

A half dozen sharp-tailed grouse burst from the undergrowth, startling me and blasting into the air, wings beating hard for a hundred yards before the birds settle again. Grouse are a key to this landscape, an indicator of how well a diminished ecosystem is thriving.

Deer leap for cover. A bald eagle stares, then lifts off a dead pine. Towhees and brown thrashers sing and flit and dash. A porcupine ambles into a small stand of trees. A homesteader family's century-old lilacs still

In late summer, jack pines are the roosting place of monarch butterflies getting ready to fly to Mexico.

bloom near what once was a farmhouse. A wolf crosses a sandy road, looks up, then vanishes in the brush.

One glorious clear morning, a crescent moon rises just before the sun, first orange then white as the world starts to glow.

On a January day, my wife and I snowshoe amid wild turkey tracks. In May, insect-eating pitcher plants poke their hungry red tubes out of the bog's bright green sphagnum moss, waiting for protein in the form of a fly. In August, monarch butterflies cluster in the jack pines, readying for the long migration to Mexico.

If I listen, I can imagine the drums of an Ojibwe summer gathering, the laughter of an end-of-winter party at a nearby log home, or even the crackling of a fire that brought tragedy to an immigrant Swedish family just down the road.

As one of many cabin owners in the region, I've been visiting the forests of northwestern Wisconsin for decades. But only in the past ten years or so have I come to treasure the barrens. Like many, I was unaware of their presence for a long time. As a friend says, "You have to be lost to find them." But since the expanse of the barrens opened for me on an idle Sunday afternoon drive, the pull has been irresistible.

I am not an expert on scrub oak trees, grouse, wolves, blueberries, history, or anything else on the barrens. And some things interest me more than others. But I've explored enough and talked to enough barrens veterans to be intrigued by the unusual fire-prone ecosystem, the desertlike wide horizons, the history and prehistory, the sense the barrens give me of both constant change and what naturalist writer Ann Zwinger once called the "infinity outside culture."

In writing this, I bring a curiosity and an urge to explore and to invite others to do the same. Come in solitude with a plant identification guide or bring friends and family to pick blueberries. Reverence for the past and for nature is helpful, and this spot by the abandoned schoolhouse is as good a place as any to appreciate how intertwined human history and natural history are. I am left with the hope that we will continue to preserve and manage the landscape well.

So what exactly are "the barrens"? First, set aside the question of whether the word is singular or plural (in this book, I say plural). And, for the blueberry-picking woman I mentioned at the beginning, we're talking about *barrens*, not *barons*.

But even so, the answer is slippery.

Indeed, some people's reaction to seeing the barrens for the first time is an exasperated "There's nothing here!" But there is plenty here. The network of plants and animals found in the barrens exists almost nowhere else in the world. This network or ecosystem, not forests of tall red pines, has been here for millennia.

At its simplest: barrens are dry landscapes of grasses, brush, and low trees, typically on sandy, nutrient-poor soil. They are susceptible to frequent fires, which they depend on. There are pine barrens and oak barrens, depending on which low tree dominates. Here, the state-owned Namekagon Barrens Wildlife Area contains both, although *pine barrens* is the term typically used.

Sometimes the terms *brush prairie* and *brush barrens* are used for this land. Savanna is another related landscape. Some people might call dry tall forests of red, white, or jack pines "barrens" because if fire were reintroduced, the land would revert to more open terrain. Others limit the word *barrens* to actively managed and protected terrain that remains open and burns regularly.

Ojibwe have long picked berries and hunted here, and Ojibwe scholar Anton Treuer suggests that the likeliest Ojibwe term for the landscape is *mitaawangaa-mashkode*—sandy prairie. When white people moved in, they built short-lived, hardscrabble communities whose residents, generations later, are sometimes referred to in local parlance as "barrens people."

Barrens tend to be flat, but landforms can vary. Low spots offer perennial water supplies and varying vegetation. Amid all the sand and sweet fern and scrub oak and jack pines at the Namekagon Barrens are bogs covered with sphagnum moss and open water surrounded by spruce and tamarack trees.

This explains why naturalists use the word *mosaic* to help define barrens. Barrens don't consist of one homogenous set of plants and animals distributed evenly across the terran. Like your bathroom tile, they come in pieces: grasses here, brush there, aging forest and interlacing fingers of other vegetation elsewhere. Unlike your bathroom tile, these pieces are constantly changing, undergoing normal forest succession and then getting "reset" by fire and other disturbances. Ecologists sometimes use the phrase *shifting mosaic* to describe the dynamic process of changing vegetation. At any rate, without fire, it's hard to have true barrens.

That's a concept some people have difficulty accepting. We've trained ourselves to fight fire—and with good reason. It has the potential to destroy property and even to injure and kill. Yet the barrens are a valuable and useful system of plants and animals that is diminished without fire. Fire has been on the land for thousands of years. As years pass without fire, it's not simply that big trees get added to the landscape, it's that other plants disappear, along with the animals that depend on those plants. It's not an easy dilemma to resolve.

The south unit features a bog some one hundred feet lower than Springbrook Trail and Namekagon Trail, ringed by tamarack and spruce.

Barrens terrain is not common: it is typically found in temperate zones where glaciers have generated huge areas of outwash sands and where fire is frequent. In the United States prior to European arrival, barrens were limited largely to areas near the Great Lakes and the Atlantic seaboard. Since then, the millions of acres that once consisted of barrens have been substantially reduced by development, agriculture, fire suppression, and forestry practices.

Some of what is left of these landscapes in the United States are pitch-pine barrens. The New Jersey Pine Barrens and New York's Albany Pine Bush are two notable examples, although these northeastern barrens tend to lack the grasses and prairie flowers of Wisconsin's barrens.

Naturalists estimate that at the time of European settlement, more than four million acres—about a tenth of today's Wisconsin—were oak and pine barrens, strung in a necklace from the northwestern to the central to the northeastern parts of the state. Today, much of that has turned to forest, the result of tree planting and the natural succession that comes with the suppression of fire. Perhaps one or two percent of the original barrens ecosystem remains, largely within a band that

The flower of the carnivorous pitcher plant stands in a sunny spot in a sphagnum bog on the south unit.

extends 150 miles from Bayfield on Lake Superior to the city of St. Croix Falls on the Wisconsin–Minnesota border.

This stretch across upper Wisconsin, known as the Northwest Sands, "has the most significant opportunity in North America to preserve, restore, and manage large scale oak/pine barrens communities," according to the Wisconsin Department of Natural Resources (DNR) master plan for the area. First, it's rare to have the collection of plants that grow on the sands of northwestern Wisconsin. Second, much of this million-acre stretch of sands is public land, owned and managed by a patchwork of county, state, and federal governments. In addition, the privately held and county-owned timber plantations here can be managed in a way that is compatible with habitat preservation.

When Europeans arrived in big numbers in the 1800s, much of the Northwest Sands consisted of mosaic landscape. Yes, there were massive old trees that attracted loggers, especially along the rivers, and, yes, mature stands of jack pine were growing across the terrain. But these jack pine stands were undergoing replacement fires every sixty to eighty years, according to Wisconsin DNR wildlife expert Ben Garrett. So there was

NORTHWEST SANDS

variety—open and treeless here, shrubby there, forested over there. More than half of the Northwest Sands was open.

Today, this land doesn't look like that in most places. Loggers cleared areas. Farmers plowed some tracts and burned others. Fires actually increased. But then foresters planted pines and suppressed fire for nearly a hundred years. Over most of these Northwest Sands, what once was open prairie or thin jack pine has become mostly forest, much of it planted for commercial harvest. What once was a habitat for grouse and prairie chickens, and even elk and bison, has grown into a dry pine woods.

And that's how many people think it should be.

And yet, over the past sixty or seventy years, a mix of wildlife managers, conservationists, and foresters have combined to manage pieces of the Northwest Sands, primarily with prescribed fires every few years but also with strategic timber cutting. They are hoping to create a big enough corridor to let the plants and animals that need the barrens maintain enough genetic diversity to thrive.

One of the most well-known of these tracts is Crex Meadows Wildlife Area. Its 30,000 acres lie at the southwest—and wettest—end of the sands, just northeast of Grantsburg, Wisconsin, and less than eighty miles from the Minneapolis–St. Paul metropolitan area across the border. The Wisconsin DNR oversees it, and its wetlands and marshes are prime country for migrating birds, including sandhill cranes, warblers, trumpeter swans, and other waterfowl.

At the other end of the sands, near Bayfield, are the hilly Moquah Barrens in the Chequamegon-Nicolet National Forest. The US Forest Service manages 22,000 acres just north of US Highway 2. In addition, Bayfield County administers 11,500 acres known as the Barnes Barrens, keeping an

Crex Meadows, a state wildlife area in the southwestern corner of the Northwest Sands, is full of lupines in summer. The flowers are much less prevalent in the drier Namekagon Barrens to the northeast. ROBERT HANSON, WDNR

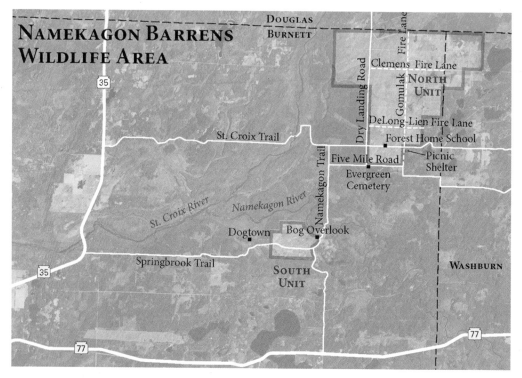

NAMEKAGON BARRENS
WILDLIFE AREA

DOUGLAS
BURNETT

Clemens Fire Lane

NORTH
UNIT

DeLong-Lien Fire Lane

St. Croix Trail

Forest Home School

Five Mile Road

Picnic
Shelter

Evergreen
Cemetery

St. Croix River

Namekagon River

Dogtown

Bog Overlook

Springbrook Trail

SOUTH
UNIT

WASHBURN

Dry Landing Road

Gomulak Fire Lane

Namekagon Trail

MAPPING SPECIALISTS, LTD.

eye on the endangered Kirtland's warbler, a bird found only in Wisconsin and Michigan that nests only in young jack pine. There are also several smaller protected pieces, including the Douglas County Wildlife Area, which consists of 4,000 acres near Gordon owned by the county and managed by the DNR.

And in the heart of the Northwest Sands lies the 6,438-acre Namekagon Barrens Wildlife Area, split into a north and a south unit separated by several miles of forest. The St. Croix and Namekagon Rivers are famous— among a handful originally protected in 1968 by the National Wild and Scenic Rivers Act. But few people visit the barrens or know anything about them, though they're just a short hike away.

After decades of managing land leased from Burnett County, the state became the owner of the wildlife area and added some adjacent acreage in Washburn County. Since 2015, it has been a state-owned management area, and in 2017 it was declared a state natural area.

The DNR (originally the Conservation Department) started clearing trees and conducting controlled burns in the 1950s to sweep away the woody growth that, if unstopped, leads to mature, tall forest. It's an exercise in keeping a forest in its earliest stages of growth. So it's good to be clear: we're not talking about pristine, untrammeled wilderness, if such a thing could actually exist. We're talking about managing the land—some would go so far as to call the result artificial—to maintain a desired state.

The barrens deserve attention partly because their rich network of plants and animals is found in relatively few places. But the human heritage on the barrens is at least thousands of years old—Indigenous stories suggest much more ancient origins—and equally compelling. There is no separating the human from the natural. For example, research by the US Forest Service shows that the number of fires hitting this landscape varied with how many people were here before, during, and after the fur trade.

In the 1950s, wildlife biologists began to manage the landscape by focusing on the sharp-tailed grouse, maintaining its habitat so it could survive. The bird is an indicator, an icon for the larger ecosystem and the web of life that includes everything from wolves to blueberries, upland sandpipers to Hill's oak, sedges to sweet fern.

Stand in the quiet on the barrens and you can cast your mind in many directions and back in time. Once, there was nothing here but ice, then virtually nothing but sand. Huge caribou and small groups of mammal-hunting Paleo-Indians walked here, carrying their stone-tipped weapons. Dakota, Ojibwe, and likely others, including Potawatomi, Ho-Chunk, and Odawa, hunted and gathered blueberries. American surveyors, loggers, land speculators, and immigrant farmers pressed in, altering the lay of the land. Wildlife biologists and foresters have tussled over it.

The Namekagon Barrens is as good a vantage point as you might want to contemplate a variety of crosscurrents pulsing through America over the centuries—from the dispossession of American Indian lands, logging booms, railroad expansion, and homesteading to the Great Depression, agricultural experimentation, immigration, and the rise of an environmental ethic. All these themes and more have played out on the barrens.

Now, again, it is mostly silent, a land of expanse, a land ruled by sand and fire.

2

Why Is the Sand Here?

To understand the barrens, think hard about sand.

Let's return to your place on St. Croix Trail by the foundation of the Forest Home School. Sand is everywhere. The road in front of you is made of it. Four-inch wolf tracks and dinosaur-like turkey and grouse prints show up clearly in it. Scoop up a handful and let it run through your fingers. Force a shovel into the ground and it's pretty much all you get—sand, with maybe a little organic material mixed in near the surface.

Hundreds of feet thick in places, sand has shaped the plants and animals that live here and governed human success and failure on the barrens.

Precipitation drains through it quickly, making the land dry and fire prone; it is poor in nutrients and supports little soil. Low-growing sweet fern and blueberries tolerate it better than other plants and have evolved strategies to thrive on it. Because the sand makes for an open country, this area served as a transportation corridor for centuries. One hundred sixty years ago, just a few feet north of where you are standing, horses drew stagecoaches across it. Later, the sand fooled agriculture experts and immigrants alike, luring homesteaders to farm but then failing to deliver on the promise of prodigious hay and vegetable crops.

Why is the sand here?

As is true everywhere on Earth, you can take the geology story way, way back. More than a billion years ago, lava erupted across this land for millions of years. The trough that someday would hold Lake Superior formed, and then sediment poured in from hundreds of miles away, cementing into sandstone.

A two-track path used by land managers as a fire break shows how sandy the barrens terrain is.

But this is no Grand Canyon or Death Valley with dozens of rock formations on display and hundreds of millions of years made plain before your eyes. All that stuff is buried. The sand piled up recently, in a geological eye blink.

The last of many glacial ages started a mere three million years ago. Sheets of miles-thick ice formed as winter snows accumulated more quickly than summer thaws could melt them. Ice covered virtually all of Canada and much of the United States. As snow and ice piled up, the mass slowly plowed south. In successive advances and retreats, glaciers inexorably ground over granite, gneiss, basalt, and sandstone. They picked up and carried huge volumes of rock and sand with them.

The geologic record of most of this era, known as the Pleistocene, is lost, erased by subsequent glaciers. But the most recent glaciation, referred to as the Wisconsinan, reached its maximum extent roughly twenty-two to twenty-six thousand years ago, according to David Ullman, who teaches geology at Northland College in nearby Ashland, Wisconsin, and whose research focuses on dating glacial movement.

Your vantage point by the schoolhouse at that time would have been buried in ice hundreds of feet thick. And so far, no sand.

But then, about twenty thousand years ago, even as ice continued to grind southward like a massive conveyer belt for rock and sediment, the southern edge of ice started melting back. As the climate slowly warmed, sediments carried hundreds of miles by the ice finally came to rest.

The retreating ice front shaped a distinctive landscape in two main ways. First, some of the sediment was dropped right where the ice melted and stayed there. But second, a lot of sediment—much of it gouged from the sandstone at the bottom of what was becoming Lake Superior—washed out onto the land. Muscular braided streams of meltwater carried this sandy mixture for miles, sorting it and piling it on top of whatever bedrock or deposits were down below. Perhaps you've seen glacial action like this in southeastern Alaska or Iceland.

Why did the sand wind up where it did? Tom Fitz, a wiry, fit-looking geology professor from Northland College and a colleague of Ullman, has been leading field trips across northern Wisconsin for years. He says you can see part of the reason right there in Ashland. The small city sits where the Bayfield Peninsula juts out into Lake Superior. Thousands of years ago, that peninsula split the last south-moving glacier into two lobes.

One lobe, the Superior, extended down across western Wisconsin to St. Croix County. A parallel lobe, the Chippewa, lay to the east. For a time, that left a spit of land between the two lobes. This became the resting place for the sands of northwestern Wisconsin, pouring in from two sides and piling up to incredible depths, the result of a quirk in the landscape that preceded the glaciers.

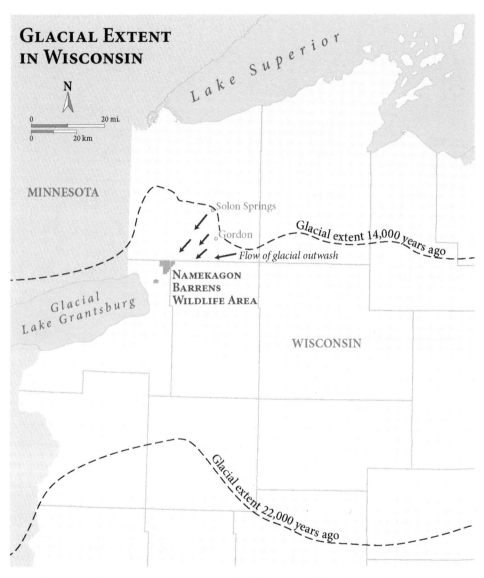

GLACIAL EXTENT IN WISCONSIN

Glacier positions are based on research by University of Wisconsin geologist Lee Clayton published in 1984. The dates are based on more recent understanding of glacial dating. MAPPING SPECIALISTS, LTD.

The ridges and low spots of the south unit show that it was formed differently from the north unit as the glaciers retreated.

One thing worth noting about all this sand, Fitz says, particularly sand carried by the Superior lobe, is that it came from bedrock rich in iron, much of it originally volcanic. As a result, white crystals of quartz became coated with iron oxide. That's why the barrens sand here has a reddish cast.

Notice how level the land is where you are on the north unit of the wildlife area. Drive a few miles across the Namekagon River to the south unit and you're in a different world, a hilly country of ridges that rise one hundred feet above bogs. Clearly these two units of the wildlife area formed differently, but how? Ullman and Fitz think it's likely the south unit formed first while the front of the glacier stood there. Ice at the toe of the glacier thrust upward, piling sediment that was then abandoned in the shape of hummocks and ridges when the glacier melted.

The glacier's toe retreated northward, and perhaps a thousand years later, the sand washing out of the glacier covered the bedrock and glacial

(*Above*) A commercial sand pit near the barrens shows both how thick the layer of sand is and how winds shaped it into dunes. DAVE WILHELM, GEOLOGICAL SOCIETY OF MINNESOTA

(*Right*) The sand of the pine barrens washed out of glaciers that scoured it from bedrock farther north. Some of this source rock was volcanic and rich in iron, which gives the barrens sand a reddish cast. LEO KENNEY

sediment in the north unit, but not the hummocks of the south unit. This north unit sand is not glacial till, which is dropped by the ice itself, but rather glacial outwash. Outwash is responsible for the look of most of the barrens.

This outwash sand, sorted by grain size and then deposited in a mostly flat layer, can be hundreds of feet thick. It is a prodigious amount of sand.

This small kettle in the north unit resulted when sand spread out on top of a big ice block. When the ice melted, the sand collapsed.

In commercial sand pits not far from the wildlife area, you can see huge wind-created sand dunes that formed after the sand was dropped. (The outwash sand has commercial uses, but its grains are too irregular in shape to be appropriate for the oil- and gas-fracking industry.)

But what about all the dips and holes you see in the flat plain, some crowded with aspen and others filled with water? In some places, you're looking at the original contours of braided streams pouring out of the glaciers. Elsewhere, you're seeing gentle undulations resulting from thousands of years of drainage since glacial times.

More dramatically, in some places—the northeast corner of the north unit, for example—this outwash sand came to rest on large blocks of ice that had broken off the glacier. When these blocks later melted, the layer of sand collapsed, forming pits or depressions twenty to thirty feet deep. Geologists also refer to these pits as *kettles*. Sometimes these pits drop below the water table, leaving open water. Others offer footholds for aspen and sedges and hiding places for deer, ducks, and other wildlife, a striking difference from the scrub oak, jack pine, and shrubs you see on most of the flat, uncollapsed plains of the barrens.

By twelve thousand years ago, the Northwest Sands were in place and Wisconsin was glacier free. Huge amounts of water drained south from

Lake Superior, carving the valley occupied today by two much smaller rivers: the north-flowing Brule and the south-flowing St. Croix.

The St. Croix forms the boundary of the Northwest Sands in many places. Northwest of the river, outside the barrens, lies hilly glacial till left by the glacier itself, marked here and there by peat bogs and volcanic bedrock. But to the river's southeast, the sand is so ubiquitous that in all those thousands of years it has failed to develop much of what most of us think of as soil. In another environment, sand would eventually mix with silt and clay to form a more fertile soil known as loam. Here, however, that material just isn't present. Rainwater and snowmelt drain right through and so do nutrients that might be present in the water. Air also filters through the sand, and the oxygen helps decompose the organic material, so even that soil component builds up very slowly on the barrens.

No matter where you are on Earth, geology is the foundation for all that exists. Here on the barrens, that means if you want to explain fire, blueberries, where the old trails ran before white people arrived, or just about anything else, you have to ask the sand.

3

The First People on the Barrens

When you walk the barrens, perhaps deer hunting along the Clemens Creek drainage in the north unit or gathering blueberries in the brush along Gomulak Fire Lane, you're doing what many, many people before you have done for a very long time.

Forever, some might say. Many American Indian creation stories, including those of the Ojibwe who still live in this region, talk about people emerging before time began, not arriving from another faraway continent. Origin stories and oral histories have gained acceptance alongside paleontology and archaeology in understanding the past, so looking at history on this land has become increasingly rich and robust.

From the perspective of Western paleontology and archaeology, humans arrived on the barrens at some point in time after the glaciers left. Paleontologists and archaeologists have for many years accepted that there is strong evidence people were living in North America some thirteen thousand years ago. More and more, scientists are accepting evidence for earlier dates.

It's hard to say exactly when people first visited the place now known as the Namekagon Barrens Wildlife Area. Archaeologists have found no evidence that the mammoth hunting of southern Wisconsin and northern Illinois extended this far north. But did people see the glaciers of Wisconsin retreating northward? No scientific evidence points to that, although Ojibwe oral history would allow for it. Did people hunt on the bare sandy tundra that the glaciers left behind? Maybe. Did they look for the woodland caribou that visited nearby lakes and wetlands that eventually formed? Almost certainly.

A painting of Ojibwe women by Eastman Johnson, based on his observations of Ojibwe people and culture during the two summers he spent at the west end of Lake Superior in 1856 and 1857. ST. LOUIS COUNTY HISTORICAL SOCIETY COLLECTION, GIFT OF RICHARD TELLER CRANE, 62.181.13

At some point, maybe ten thousand years ago, somebody likely walked past your schoolhouse perch. The late Paleo-Indians—the term archaeologists use for the last stage of the continent's earliest inhabitants, people living until about that time—had gradually moved north. They were following plants and animals in a warming climate. Moving in small bands, people entered a land of spruce forests, sedges, grasses, and wetlands. They hunted with thrusting spears and atlatls, gathered plants, and

Sedges fill a pond at the head of a ravine that leads to Clemens Creek.

fished. They carried stone tools for hundreds of miles, some of the stone coming from the south and some from north of Lake Superior, leaving evidence of a mobile hunter-gatherer society.

Studies of pollen in lake sediments indicate that lakes and wetlands formed after glaciers left, attracting woodland caribou, waterfowl, and fish. John Lambert, an archaeologist at the Illinois State Archaeological Survey, suggests that human hunters were soon in pursuit. Lambert also speculates that it is possible people were in the barrens area before then, but for such brief, infrequent visits or in such low numbers that they are just not "archaeologically visible" today.

About twenty miles from the Namekagon Barrens, at the towns of Solon Springs and Gordon, are two sites archaeologists researched in the 1980s and 1990s, responding to plans for widening US Highway 53 and extending a sewer line. One is known as the Sucices site in Solon Springs; the other is the Bowling Lane site in Gordon.

This
Paleo-Indian
spearpoint, found at
an archaeological site at
Squirrel Dam about 125 miles east
of the Namekagon Barrens, is evidence
that people were in northern Wisconsin some
ten thousand years ago LOGAN MUSEUM OF
ANTHROPOLOGY, BELOIT COLLEGE

Researchers at both sites—Lambert at Sucices and Norman Haywood of the Burnett County Historical Society at Bowling Lane—recovered a number of stone tools, leading them to conclude that late Paleo-Indians were hunting and gathering in the area close to ten thousand years ago. They found stone points fashioned from a distinctive hard sandstone that was quarried about 150 miles away. Several artifacts suggest that people were sewing leather garments and perhaps fashioning dugout canoes from spruce or pine logs, according to Lambert's research. Were these the first visitors to the nearby barrens?

Lambert thinks that's a good guess and finds it especially impressive how far—hundreds of miles—people seemed to be roaming from north to south through the year, evidence of substantial planning. They may not have had calendars, but they knew where they wanted to be and when.

Eventually people intensified the search for food to satisfy growing populations. As the Paleo-Indian era shifted to the Archaic, fishing became more important, as did wild rice harvesting. Technology like fish weirs and copper tools would have changed lives. Later, the bow and arrow made hunting more effective. A thousand years ago, ancestors of Dakota people were likely responsible for burial mounds near Yellow Lake, not far from the barrens. By 1600, if you were standing near the schoolhouse site and heard someone talking as they picked blueberries or hazelnuts nearby, there's a good chance the language would have been

Dakota. Dakota people were in what is now Wisconsin long before contact
with Europeans, as were other nations, including Kickapoo, Wyandot,
Potawatomi, Odawa, and Ho-Chunk. In the area now including the barrens, Dakota and Ojibwe were the most prevalent in recent centuries.

It's possible the Dakota people cultivated corn, but they would have
moved throughout the year to hunt, fish, and gather berries. At that point,
they likely were not using iron, but they would soon encounter it.

Ojibwe people migrating from the east were equipped with iron kettles,
knives, guns, and other new technology. Beginning around 1650 in this
area, the longstanding culture changed and a new economy formed. A new
force, the French fur trade, was on the land, and the Ojibwe (also known as
Chippewa and by the name the people call themselves, Anishinaabe) were
full partners. "The French were evidently the first white men to establish
themselves among the Chippewa," Ojibwe tribal member Jerome Arbuckle
wrote hundreds of years later for a government-sponsored collection of
essays about northern Wisconsin Ojibwe history. "They were the first, last
and only white nation that ever gained the full confidence and complete
good will of the Chippewa tribe in its entirety. In contrast to other white
usurpers, the French made no attempt to extort huge cessions of land from
the Indians or to dispossess the aboriginal inhabitants."

How the Ojibwe and the Dakota interacted as this shift took place was
neither simple nor constant. Over the years, they lived with each other,
benefited from each other, and, at times, fought one another.

The Anishinaabe people likely emerged as a distinct culture some two
or three thousand years ago on the Atlantic coast, according to Ojibwe
scholar Anton Treuer. In Ojibwe oral history, prophets provided the people
with a set of predictions known as the Seven Fires, each fire representing
a period of time in the people's westward migration. Ultimately, the prophets said, the people would find "the land where food grows on water," a
reference to wild rice.

After centuries of movement, by the mid-1600s many Ojibwe people
lived at what is now Sault Saint Marie at the east end of Lake Superior, a
place that became a hub of trade with the French. Then in 1679, Ojibwe and
Dakota leaders agreed that the Ojibwe would obtain hunting and settlement
rights throughout what would become northern Wisconsin. They would

act as fur trade middlemen between the Dakota and the French, an arrangement that led to prosperity for a time for both Dakota and Ojibwe peoples.

Madeline Island, near what is now Bayfield, had already emerged as a spiritual center for many Ojibwe, considered the final stopping place in the people's centuries-long westward migration. It grew into a significant post in the fur trade. Eventually, Ojibwe villages formed along Lake Superior and elsewhere, including the mouth of the Yellow River, where Danbury sits today not far from the barrens.

According to the St. Croix Chippewa Indians of Wisconsin—the band whose reservation is closest to the Namekagon Barrens today—the Marten clan of Ojibwe came into an area of valuable resources along the St. Croix River in what became Burnett, Douglas, and Washburn Counties.

Treuer argues that many people today don't realize the harmony and prosperity that existed between the Dakota and Ojibwe into the 1730s. And indeed, today many claim heritage from both tribes. But eventually tensions built, largely as a result of shifting alliances and territorial maneuvering

An 1850s lithograph by Henry Lewis shows Ojibwe people building shelters.
LIBRARY OF CONGRESS LC-2019630566

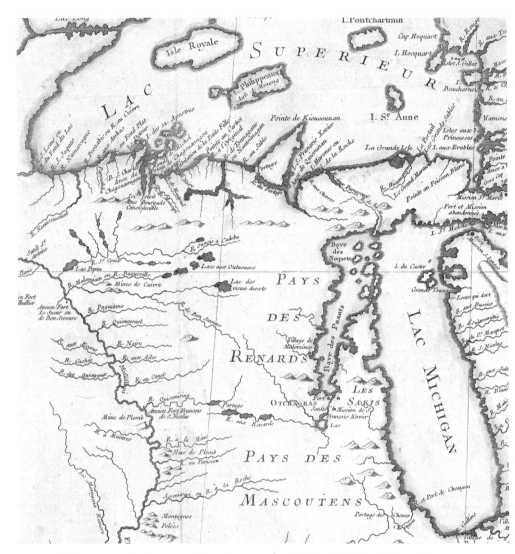

This 1755 map depicts part of New France at the height of the French fur trade.
WISCONSIN DIGITAL COLLECTIONS

by the French and the British. During the second half of the 1700s, the barrens and the surrounding territory were a war zone, although the relationships among people were complicated. The groups might hunt together and intermarry in the fall and winter and then fight in the summer.

In the meantime, the Namekagon Barrens made up part of the "seasonal rounds"—the way of life for Ojibwe people that was generations old even in the midst of a changing economy. Florina Denomie, a member of the Bad River tribe on Lake Superior, wrote in the 1930s that "the Chippewa of early days moved from place to place as the seasons changed; hence permanent Chippewa settlements were practically unknown."

In the fall and winter, people would hunt and trap in the woods, where they could find fuel for warmth. In March they would move to a sugar camp to tap maple trees and boil sap for sugar. That was a time for gathering birch and cedar bark, as well as roots and plants used in medicines. Then came fish camps along the rivers. According to Dawn White, a treaty resource specialist for the Great Lakes Indian Fish & Wildlife Commission, the name *Namekagon* is Ojibwe for "river at the place of many sturgeon," a reference to the huge fish that still ply the namesake river. By summer the people would be foraging on the barrens, picking and drying blueberries.

As plants matured in late summer and into fall, many that are still plentiful on the barrens today were gathered for use as medicines. According

The pristine and well-known Namekagon River flows right past the Namekagon Barrens Wildlife Area.

New Jersey tea grows throughout the barrens.

to Denomie and other tribal members writing in the 1930s, hazelnuts were both a food and a source of medicine. Low-growing wintergreen was used as a liniment to treat rheumatism. Sweet fern could be made into an infusion taken for colic and diarrhea. The roots of wild roses yielded an eyewash. And New Jersey tea, a flowering plant, became an ingredient in many medicines, especially those treating lung problems.

And, of course, as fall arrived, the people came to nearby lakes to harvest wild rice, an activity that continues today among the St. Croix Ojibwe. The Ojibwe in this area were known as "Folle Avoines" after the French phrase for wild rice, according to a tribal account of the history.

The mobile life of hunting and gathering was portrayed in the book *Cecilia*, a reminiscence by Lafayette Connor about his Ojibwe grandmother. Connor was writing many years later about a time he didn't actually witness, but he describes his grandmother's journey as a young child in 1839. According to Connor, the family of Odigomokwe Hollowfoot (Cecilia Connor) spent that winter in "sugar camp" west of Lake Superior. They canoed down the St. Louis River, along the southern shore of the big lake, and up the Brule River. Then, with their canoes patched, they headed down the St. Croix to Big Fish Rapids, a fishing camp about a mile west of the present-day Namekagon Barrens. Camp there lasted through June as the people caught and smoked fish, and then they moved again, dividing into smaller family groups.

Connor says Cecilia's group went down the St. Croix a few miles to the Yellow River and then up Loon Creek to camp in an area a few miles south of today's wildlife area. Here was good territory for wild rice and blueberries. Eventually, as the summer passed, they reversed course and headed back up the St. Croix, down the Brule, and along the shore of Lake Superior to return to winter camp in what is now Minnesota. Regardless of whether Connor really knew all the details of his grandmother's life when she was a little girl, his chronicle provides the gist of life at the time.

In the 1825 Treaty of Prairie du Chien, the US government drew a line on the map that formally divided Dakota and Ojibwe land. In the eyes of the United States, the barrens country belonged to the Ojibwe. One of the signers was Kabemabe, a leader at a village near what is now the Gordon Flowage northeast of the barrens and a man whose influence is said to have reached the Namekagon River.

Former Wisconsin state archaeologist Robert Birmingham, who directed research in the 1980s at a site near the wildlife area, concluded that by the 1830s, the Ojibwe had established villages throughout the upper St. Croix River drainage area. These villages had their underpinnings in wild rice, berries, maple sugar, fish, wild game, and even some corn, bean, pumpkin, and potato gardening. But it was a time of disruption and difficulty, partly because of diseases transmitted through European contact, partly because of unusually cold weather in the 1830s, and partly because of the demise of the fur trade, which moved west as fur-bearing animals were trapped out and changes in fashion lessened demand for beaver. The steady westward push of Europeans into the heart of North America meant that again the economy of the land was about to be reshaped.

4

TREATY WRITERS AND
SURVEYORS ARRIVE

The American treaty era had begun.

Where once you might have heard the conversation of Dakota and Ojibwe hunter-gatherers, you were soon to hear the sounds of lumbering and the movement of horse-drawn wagons and stagecoaches.

In the 1783 Treaty of Paris, which ended the Revolutionary War, the land destined to become Wisconsin fell under the sovereignty of the United States (not that the people living near the barrens would have paid much notice). As colonists and settlers moved west into American Indian country, the US government carved out territories and states. On the map, the barrens were part of Illinois Territory, then Michigan Territory, and finally Wisconsin Territory. On the actual ground, the land remained in the hands of the Ojibwe.

Timber interests, not settlers, were the driving force to change that. Demand for cheap pine was booming in towns along the Mississippi River, and transporting lumber from New York and Pennsylvania was prohibitively expensive. American businessmen were eager to get their hands on the trees lining the St. Croix, the Namekagon, and other tributary rivers east of the Mississippi.

Entrepreneurs started buying and stealing timber from the Ojibwe, and then, in 1837, the Pine Tree Treaty was signed by representatives of the United States and more than a dozen Ojibwe chiefs and warriors. The treaty ceded to the federal government a huge swath of what would become Wisconsin and Minnesota, and the Namekagon Barrens were in the middle of it.

Much is unclear about the treaty negotiations, which took place over several days in July 1837 near the mouth of what is now the Minnesota River at Mendota. Territorial governor Henry Dodge led the talks for the Americans and pressed for a quick signing. Ojibwe chiefs from land that later became Minnesota were involved from the start, but leaders from the Wisconsin land arrived later and apparently were less active in the negotiation that took place.

Ojibwe leaders agreed not to the outright sale of land but to sharing it, according to Anton Treuer. Interpretation was difficult and the Ojibwe kept no written account of what happened. For example, Treuer points out, silence on the part of some leaders would have been interpreted in the Ojibwe culture as declining to agree. For the Americans, failure to object meant agreement.

It therefore seems likely that this treaty joined the long list of those in which American Indians were pressured or otherwise left with a disadvantage as eager traders wielded influence. It was not long before a number of Wisconsin Ojibwe leaders complained to President Martin Van Buren that they had not been compensated fairly and that traders had taken advantage of them.

The 1837 treaty did not call for the Ojibwe to move, and it specifically preserved their hunting, fishing, and wild ricing rights in the ceded territory, rights that were reaffirmed by the US Supreme Court in 1999 after a lengthy legal battle. But in 1850, the government did make an effort to push the Ojibwe people from Wisconsin, requiring those collecting promised annuities to travel not to the Indian agency on Madeline Island in Lake Superior but to Big Sandy Lake in Minnesota Territory. There they had to wait through harsh winter weather before trying to return home. Hundreds of Ojibwe died, mostly from measles, dysentery, or exposure.

"Our women and children do indeed cry, our Father, on account of their suffering from cold and hunger," Chief Buffalo, a leader among Lake Superior Ojibwe, wrote to the commissioner of Indian Affairs in 1851.

The next spring, at age ninety-three, Chief Buffalo and others traveled by foot, canoe, and rail from Madeleine Island to Washington—on their

PINE TREE TREATY (1837)

Ojibwe cessions

MAPPING SPECIALISTS, LTD.

return trip they likely walked the Northwest Sands right past your spot by the former school house—to push President Millard Fillmore to let them remain in Wisconsin.

In 1854, the US government recognized several bands of Ojibwe and created reservations for them. It was not until 1934 that the government recognized the St. Croix band of Ojibwe. Once known as the "lost tribe," the St. Croix today has a reservation of some four thousand acres broken into small tracts in Burnett, Douglas, Barron, and Polk Counties. About two thousand people live on the reservation.

(*Facing page*) The first page of the 1837 Pine Tree Treaty between the US government and Ojibwe leaders from areas that later became parts of Minnesota and Wisconsin. Article 1 calls for the cession of land by the Ojibwe; Article 2 lists annuity payments and other agreements. NATIONAL ARCHIVES 68144559

Articles of a Treaty made and concluded at St Peters

(the confluence of the St Peters and Mississippi Rivers) in the Territory of Wisconsin between The United States of America, by their Commissioner HENry Dodge, Governor of said Territory, and the Chippewa Nation of Indians, by their Chiefs and Head Men.

Article 1. The said Chippewa Nation, cede to the United States, all that Tract of country, included within the following boundaries: BEGinning at the junction of the Crow Wing and Mississippi Rivers, between Twenty and thirty miles above where the Mississippi is crossed by the Forty sixth parallel of North Latitude, and running thence to the north point of Lake St Croix, one of the sources of the St Croix River; thence to and along the dividing Ridge between the waters of Lake Superior and those of the Mississippi, to the sources of the Ocha Sua Sepe a tributary of the Chippewa River; thence to a point on the Chippewa River Twenty miles below the out let of Lake De Flambeau; thence to the junction of the Wisconsin and Pelican Rivers; thence on an East course Twenty Five miles; thence southerly, on a course parallel with that of the Wisconsin River, to the line dividing the Territories of the Chippewas and Menomonies; thence to the Plover Portage; thence along the southern boundary of the Chippewa country, to the commencement of the boundary line dividing it from that of the Sioux, half a days march below the Falls on the Chippewa River; thence with said boundary line to the mouth of Wah-tap River, at its junction with the Mississippi; & thence up the Mississippi to the place of beginning.

Article 2. In consideration of the cession aforesaid, The United States agree to make to the Chippewa Nation, annually, for the term of Twenty Years, from the date of the ratification of this Treaty, the following payments.

1. Nine Thousand Five Hundred Dollars, to be paid in money.
2. Nineteen Thousand Dollars to be delivered in goods.
3. Three Thousand Dollars, for establishing Three Black Smiths shops, supporting the Black Smiths, & furnishing them with Iron and Steel.
4. One Thousand Dollars for Farmers, and for supplying them and the Indians, with implements of labor, with grain or seed; and whatever else may be necessary to enable them, to carry on their Agricultural pursuits.
5. Two Thousand Dollars in Provisions
6. Five Hundred Dollars in Tobacco.

The Provisions and Tobacco, to be delivered at the same time with the goods, and the money to be paid; which time, or times, as well as the place or places, where they are to be delivered, shall be fixed upon under the direction of the President of The United States.

The Black Smiths shops to be placed at such points in the Chippewa country, as shall be designated by the Superintendent of Indian Affairs, or under his direction.

Members of what is now the Bad River band of Ojibwe gather in 1852 at La Pointe, waiting for their annuity payments. This was two years after the government forced the Ojibwe to travel to Minnesota for their promised payments. WHI IMAGE ID 109506

What the 1837 treaty did do was give formal entrée to timber interests. Entrepreneurs flooded into the region. Among those taking advantage was Henry Sibley, a fur trader who signed the treaty as a witness and who would eventually become Minnesota's first governor and lead the military expedition against the Dakota in the US–Dakota War of 1862.

Loggers claimed some of the land in and around what has become the wildlife area. Later, the government granted large tracts of land to a railroad company as an incentive to build railroads. Homesteaders claimed smaller chunks or bought directly from the US government. These settlers, largely of European descent, paid little regard to the rights the Ojibwe had retained.

As they had when the fur trade with Europeans began, Ojibwe both maintained traditions and adapted to a new economy based on timber and labor for hire. Many engaged in the logging that quickly dominated in the second half of the 1800s, focusing on the river valleys of the St. Croix, Namekagon, Totogatic, and others. The turn of the century was a wrenching time for the Ojibwe. The population was at a low point, Ojibwe historian Brenda Child notes, calling their experience over the following years "a catastrophic dispossession."

The American Push

Loggers went after the big white pines first, both because they were huge and because they were lighter in weight and easier to float to sawmills downriver. Red pines, jack pines, and eventually hardwood trees also appealed to those in the timber industry.

The logging settlements of Stillwater and St. Croix Falls formed quickly, and land along the St. Croix River right next to what is now the Namekagon Barrens Wildlife Area was being logged by 1855. Loggers periodically dammed the river to raise water levels and float the logs to mills downstream.

But land nearby, destined to someday become the barrens wildlife area, was more open, not necessarily a big draw for loggers right away. This was the shape-shifting "mosaic" I discuss in the first chapter.

In 1837, the year of the Pine Tree treaty, an itinerant Methodist minister and future Indian agent named Alfred Brunson wrote to the brand-new Wisconsin territorial legislature to describe the territory's land. Here's his

Logs jam the St. Croix River in 1895, the peak of logging in the area around the barrens. WHI IMAGE ID 62818

discussion of the Northwest Sands, starting near Lake Superior: "A little west of La Pointe, and 10 or 12 miles south of the lake shore, the prairie country commences, which extends to and beyond the St. Croix and the Mississippi, and offers great inducements to agriculturalists who like such a high north latitude."

There's debate over exactly how forested the barrens terrain was at that point. How much was open? How much was patchy jack pine forest? How much resemblance is there between what we see today and what was there almost two hundred years ago? These are tricky questions to answer because they involve a moving target.

A big clue comes from a man named Hiram C. Fellows. Once treaties were signed and land taken, the government contracted with surveyors— including Fellows—to mark and label the townships and section squares on which all subsequent land deals depended. On the last day of September 1855, Fellows led a small crew into what many years later would become Blaine Township on the northern end of Burnett County. Fellows and his crew—two chainmen and an axeman—marked section lines and described the soils, terrain, and trees in each. Just weeks earlier, a similar crew led by Albert Stuntz had surveyed the township lines. Fellows's job was to fill in the details.

The six-mile square he worked has been known ever since as Township 42 North, Range 14 West, and it is cleaved in two by the St. Croix River. Fellows wrote in his notebook that west of the river, this land was "heavily timbered with good white pine." Furthermore, a logging company had claimed land even before Fellows got there and was felling trees and building a dam on the river. East of the river, though, where the wildlife area lies today, Fellows noted the sandy soils were "thinly timbered with black [jack] pine."

Good survey crew practice was to drive four-by-four-inch posts two feet long into the ground to mark section corners. Surveyors would then mark and record the size of two nearby "bearing trees," noting the direction, or "bearing," from the post to the tree. In this way, they could guide future land buyers to the survey markers. Near the rivers, these bearing trees were typically a short distance from the survey posts, and often they were white pines twenty-five to thirty inches in diameter.

On the barrens, it was a different story.

Take your spot by the schoolhouse. When Fellows and his crew set up their equipment here more than a century and a half ago, the nearest bearing trees were eighteen-inch-diameter red pines nearly four hundred feet away. A half mile east, at the corner of what is now St. Croix Trail and Gomulak Fire Lane, the nearest bearing trees were jack pines six and ten inches in diameter some 250 feet from that post. And a survey post in the other direction had only one bearing tree. "No other near," Fellows noted.

Surveyors like Fellows undoubtedly varied in their thoroughness and may have defined their terms inconsistently. To be sure, in some places on the barrens, Fellows's bearing trees were closer to the marker and indicated mature stands of jack pine. The vegetation could vary substantially.

But twenty years later, geologist E. T. Sweet reported much the same: "The barrens have a timber growth exclusively their own. The trees are either scrub pines or black-jack oaks, averaging in diameter about three or four inches and in height not over 15 feet."

A survey of Wisconsin geology in the 1870s defined the shifting mosaic this way: "Fire has killed the timber over wide areas, on which grass was growing, exhibiting before our eyes nature's simple method of converting woodland into prairie. The reverse process is just as simple. When prairies are no longer swept over by fire, timber springs up, reconverting prairie into woodland. Grass, with fire as an ally, can beat timber. Timber can beat grass when it has no fire to fight."

Clearly, the barrens were not like the thick red- and white-pine forests growing across much of northern Wisconsin today. You stand today in the managed wildlife area and see a land that is probably not identical to what Fellows saw, but it is reasonably close. You have to look four hundred feet or more to find a tree of good size and you can understand why, again and again, surveyors like Fellows labeled this land "pine barrens" with "3rd rate soil."

Recent analysis of these surveys has led ecologists to conclude that entire quarter sections, a half mile on each side, were sometimes treeless. In other places, trees were spaced out every 150 to 1,500 feet. In the Northwest Sands as a whole, ecologists estimate there were only about ten trees per acre in the mid-1800s, far fewer than the number growing today after more than a century of fire suppression and tree planting.

In his notes from the 1855 survey, Hiram Fellows reported on his crew marking the spot on the barrens where the Forest Home School would be built a half century later. Two bearing trees were listed to guide future surveyors to the spot, a yellow (red) pine 523 links (344 feet) to the southwest and another one 607 links (400 feet) to the northwest. He considered the land surface "level" and the soil "3rd rate." COURTESY OF THE WISCONSIN BOARD OF COMMISSIONERS OF PUBLIC LANDS

Jack pines proliferate on the barrens.

This map, created by Robert Finley in 1976, shows the vegetation in northwestern Wisconsin in the mid-1800s, when settlers arrived from the eastern United States and Europe. The tan represents a land of jack pine, scrub oak, and barrens, and you can see how closely it reflects the presence of the Northwest Sands. The region's famous white and red pines show up as dark green on either side of the jack pine and scrub oak barrens areas. WISCONSIN DEPARTMENT OF NATURAL RESOURCES

WHITE PINE, RED PINE

JACK PINE

WHITE BIRCH, ASPEN

JACK PINE BARRENS

JACK PINE - SCRUB OAK BARRENS

JACK PINE, SCRUB OAK

ENTER THE STAGECOACH

Fellows and his crew were a vanguard, of course. By the time he made his survey in 1855, a road already cut through the barrens, connecting Lake Superior with St. Paul. Dakota, Ojibwe, and other American Indians had likely originated the route, using the open sandy terrain to travel great distances. Brian Finstad, a longtime student of barrens history from Gordon, has suggested that walking the sands might well have been easier most of the year than taking the more fabled water route of the Brule and St. Croix Rivers.

Finstad's research shows that by the 1860s, the road was carrying wagons, mail, and regularly scheduled stagecoaches on a route that took it right past where the schoolhouse would be built some forty years later. In 1863, the Minnesota Stage Company built a bridge across the Namekagon River squarely between what are now the two units of the wildlife area. Gone now for many years, the bridge was downstream and around a bend from where the modern steel bridge carries the traffic of Namekagon Trail, the road that spans the river. Many modern-day canoeists have unknowingly passed the old bridge site as they paddled toward the St. Croix.

Among the first to use the new bridge was the family of Robert and Anna Minturn, wealthy New Yorkers on a several-week camping excursion to the wild lands of Minnesota and Wisconsin. In December 1863, *Harper's Magazine* published a long travelogue describing their journey via wagon from St. Paul to Bayfield.

The magazine story carried no byline, but Spooner historian Don Monson, who compiled a book on the bridge and the road, thinks it was written by the couple's eighteen-year-old daughter, Sarah. It describes the trip as high adventure and notes that shortly after setting out from the posh International Hotel in downtown St. Paul, the entourage considered turning back and instead taking a trip on a riverboat down the Mississippi. But they carried on toward Lake Superior, encountering Ojibwe, a few white people, and only a half dozen other wagons along the way.

Sarah duly reported the road's deep sand, the dryness resulting from a two-month drought, and even a wildfire the group rolled through in the vicinity of what is now the wildlife area. "Trees and grass in flames seemed

Ruts remain on the north unit from the stagecoach road built in the 1850s.

to surround us," she wrote. "As we drove on, the fire extended to the right and left. The conductor rushed ahead, knocking over one or two charred trees, one falling but a moment before the carriage reached the spot."

The description provides evidence that in a land frequently visited by fire, no given fire burned especially hot or out of control. This contrasts with the large and destructive fires that later roared through timber land.

As the group continued north, Minturn captured well the mosaic of a changing barrens, from "numberless evergreens" to "acres overgrown with young pines and balsam firs"—probably a mistaken reference to jack pines—to charred areas with "no signs of vegetation."

Today, especially in spring before vegetation is thick or after one of the area's controlled burns, you can see the ruts wagons made on this stagecoach road. It takes a practiced eye to spot these subtle tracks, and Finstad, who is passionate about the road and its history, is particularly adept at spotting them.

The Minturn family apparently took its trip at the instigation of Henry Rice, one of Minnesota's first US senators, a land speculator along the stagecoach road and founder of the town of Bayfield. Rice bought land at more than a half dozen places along this road, including a key two hundred acres at the site of the bridge, land that today is adjacent to the south unit of the wildlife area. He was instrumental in building the bridge over the Namekagon. A post office operated at the bridge for a short time, and eventually a man named George Moores ran a farm and stopping place near the river, serving travelers and those working for logging operations.

By the 1880s, railroad travel caused the road to fade into the sand. Logging peaked by the 1890s. The boom had cleared forests; dams and erosion had damaged wild rice areas and reduced fish populations. But timber slash fires opened land, and blueberries became a commercial crop for some.

Through all of this, the Ojibwe continued to hunt, harvest rice, collect maple sap, fish, find herbs and roots for traditional medicines, and pick berries. Many took jobs in sawmills and logging camps, laboring as part of the cash economy. The last Ojibwe settlement near what became the wildlife area was a place called Dogtown on Dogtown Creek where the short stream runs into the Namekagon. Today this is an uninhabited spot just west of the south unit of the wildlife area, at Springbrook Trail.

In 1982, Wisconsin state archaeologist Robert Birmingham directed research sponsored by the Burnett County Historical Society to learn more about this community. Among the findings was that by the 1910s and 1920s, Dogtown had dwindled to two families—the Kenebecs and the Carlsons. Others had moved to Danbury, old-timers told Birmingham. Indeed, the population of Great Lakes–area Ojibwe reached its lowest point around 1900.

Even so, Dogtown was the site of large gatherings in the summers to pick blueberries on the barrens. This was a continuation of berry picking as a practice central to the traditional economies of Ojibwe people, according to Chantal Norrgard, a scholar of Ojibwe people in northern Minnesota and Wisconsin. Berrying was an example of people using traditional activities as a means to avoid pressure to farm and thus fit more snugly into the white economy.

Blueberry picking has long been an important Ojibwe activity in northern Wisconsin. This group gathered in 1910 to pick in Barron County south of the barrens. WHI IMAGE ID 79031

From the Great Depression until World War II, Ojibwe people would gather in large camps to pick throughout northern Wisconsin, a means of making money and renewing social contact. According to Norrgard, by that time, there was less emphasis on traditional drying and preserving and more on the commercial opportunity, supplying, for example, a bakery in Duluth and other wild fruit buyers.

A 1938 government survey in Minnesota said an Ojibwe family might pick as much as twenty-four quarts a day when the season was on. Bad River tribal member Florina Denomie pointed out the social value of picking: "You are living in the open, where the children romp and play, and sleeping in a tent at night you have the advantage of breathing only the purest air. The berry fields hold out to you improved health conditions, recreation for your children, and while you may come to the berry fields rather sun burned and a shade darker, you feel better in every way."

John Kenebec, an Ojibwe man identified in several federal censuses in the early 1900s, is believed to have been the last resident of Dogtown, living near the mouth of Dogtown Creek until he died in the late 1930s, a century after the Pine Tree Treaty was signed and just a few years after the St. Croix tribe was recognized by the federal government. Some area residents that archaeologist Birmingham's researchers talked to remembered Kenebec working in logging camps; one census identified him as a day laborer, another as a farmer. He spoke English; his family members spoke only Anishinaabe, according to the census. It seems likely he was among the many Ojibwe trying to straddle the divide between cultures.

Kenebec's father, George Kenebec, had homesteaded 160 acres along Dogtown Creek. When George died in 1917, his homestead was divided among three children. Two of them sold their shares the next year, but John held on to his fifty-three acres on Dogtown Creek until he died. Some of the land is now owned by Burnett County, and the rest is divided among a half dozen private owners just west of the wildlife area's south unit.

Descendants of those who hunted and gathered on the barrens are still present, of course, some continuing to hunt and gather there. Many live in the Danbury-Webster-Spooner area, and the bands of Lake Superior Chippewa consult frequently with a variety of state and federal agencies on the historic, cultural, and natural resources of the Northwest Sands.

Webster resident John Jensen remembers picking blueberries as a child on the day humans landed on the moon in 1969. Jensen, whose grandfather was Ojibwe, also remembers hunting deer, and even sharp-tailed grouse, on the barrens in the 1970s. He still comes back to the barrens even though he doesn't hunt any more. What it gives him, he says, is a sense of timelessness.

5

FARMS ON THE SAND

L ook closely around the barrens and you can see a few signs of agriculture. Bases of circular concrete silos hide in the brush; a square patch of vegetation may appear a little out of place; a lilac blooms in what otherwise is pine and oak woods; an odd depression might contain a few pieces of broken crockery that once belonged to a farming family.

By the early twentieth century, the barrens were attracting farmers, apparently a second-chancer's dream. That land by the schoolhouse once was farmed by a young couple named Benjamin and Ruby Hillock. He was from Iowa, she from southern Wisconsin. Their neighbors were Charlie and Bertena Krause, a young couple who left Milwaukee to start a family on the barrens. Nearby lived a large family of Swedish immigrants, Arvid and Augusta Lyons and their eleven children. They and others came to the barrens in the early 1900s after business and government leaders declared that agriculture could replace the declining logging industry.

It wouldn't take long to learn how wrong that prediction was. Before 1920, the Hillocks had moved to Missouri, then Arkansas, then New Mexico and Texas. The Krauses were back in Milwaukee. Arvid and Augusta Lyons were dead, their children scattered.

For decades, the westward movement of Americans looking for land had focused on the prairies of the Midwest, bypassing the northern forests. But as timber was exhausted, land that had been ceded in treaties to the federal government opened for homesteading and for purchase. Farmers could buy land from the federal government, from railroads that had been

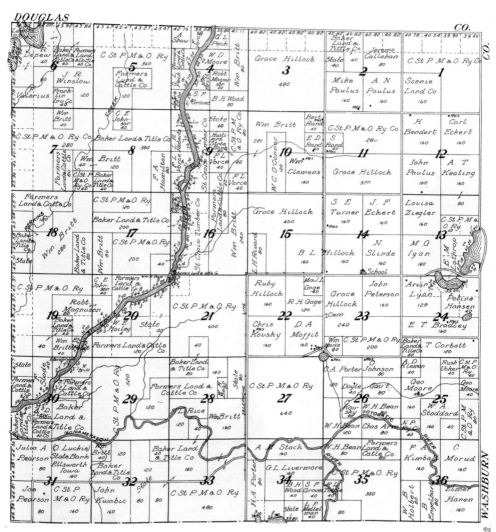

This historic plat map shows land ownership in 1915 in part of Blaine Township.
What is today the wildlife area lies mostly in the northeast quarter of the map.
The Chicago, St. Paul, Minneapolis & Omaha Railway still owned pieces, but much
of the land was in the hands of the Hillock, Paulus, Turner, and Eckert families.

granted vast acreages, and from multitudes of land companies created to peddle the former timberlands.

State leaders, local businesses, academics, and a steady stream of promoters all joined the cry to farm northern Wisconsin, including the barrens. In 1895, the Wisconsin legislature commissioned a guide to farming in northern Wisconsin, to be prepared by the dean of the University of Wisconsin's college of agriculture, William Henry. Under Henry's direction, several university professors set out in the summer of 1895 to canvass the state's northern counties. With promotion their clear aim, they found "marvelously fine crops."

Henry described the soils and climates, predicted which crops might be profitable, and laid out what he saw as a great opportunity to draw "a desirable class of farmers" to northern Wisconsin. "There is already a goodly tide of settlers flowing into northern Wisconsin," the guide said. "If it accomplishes its designed purpose this book will swell the number materially, bringing to us an intelligent, worthy class of people who are posted in advance on the kind of country they are coming to and who, knowing this, are not likely to leave us disappointed after a few years' stay."

Land was cheap. A farmer could sell a small plot of land in southern Wisconsin and buy a much larger stake in the north. Yes, the climate could be hot in summer and cold in winter but not as inhospitable as it would be without the moderating influence of Lakes Superior and Michigan, the handbook promised.

As it happened, a severe frost in May 1895 greatly damaged the grass crop across the northern United States, but this was unusual, according to the report: "Northern Wisconsin will always be known for its splendid timothy hay." The report compared the sandy soils of Burnett and other counties to the truck farms of Long Island, New Jersey, and Maryland, adapted to growing early vegetables. It noted the challenges of the light soils lacking nutrients but suggested crop rotations and sheep grazing. It predicted that potatoes and garden vegetables "can undoubtedly be produced on these lands of excellent quality and in paying quantities."

In addition to the handbook, Henry generated articles for publication in regional newspapers. According to historian Arlen Helgeson, "In spite of the predominant sand and swamp of Burnett County, [Henry] had no hesitation predicting that it will become one of the most prosperous regions in all Wisconsin and that in a short time all the lands will be taken up and most of them cleared into good farms."

Railroads, private land companies, and newspapers promoted northern Wisconsin, many making extravagant claims about the land. The question of how good or poor the land might be for farming had actually come up much earlier. Back in 1837, when Henry Dodge, governor of Wisconsin Territory, was negotiating the treaty that transferred Ojibwe land to the US government, he purposely downplayed the agricultural significance of the land, claiming that it had no value to farmers and so was not worth as much money as the Ojibwe sought.

An Ojibwe leader named La Trappe caught Dodge at his game and corrected him with these words: "We understand you, that you have been told our country is no good to cultivate. It is false. There is no better soil to cultivate than it, *until you get up to where the pine region commences* [italics added]." The Ojibwe knew where there was good farmland and where there wasn't. But the search for farmers was on, extending to other parts of Wisconsin, the rest of the Midwest, and Europe. A state board of immigration was established in 1899 to bring farmers to northern Wisconsin. Counties, including Burnett, followed suit, establishing immigration commissions of their own.

Pounding the drum of immigration more heavily than anyone else was Ed Peet. The son of an itinerant Methodist preacher, Peet was part journalist, part showman. For a while, he was an advance man for traveling entertainment troupes; at other times, he traded in real estate. Peet also founded the *Journal of Burnett County* and headed the county's board of immigration.

In 1902, he reported that northern farmers were experimenting with peanuts, alfalfa, and broomcorn: "The outcome of these efforts is being watched with much interest. Should it be found that any one of the above-named commodities could be successfully produced in this county it would mark it as destined to soon become one of the most wealthy counties in the northern part of Wisconsin." Peet bragged that while dry conditions plagued crops elsewhere, "they were fresh and green here [northern Burnett County]. During these times of drouths at no time was the earth dry more than two inches below the surface. . . . With few exceptions, the lands of northern Burnett County are free from stones." Furthermore, he declared, the swamps of Burnett County were virtually free of poisonous snakes.

Peet was correct about the stones and the snakes, but you might wonder about his claims for the moisture in the sand. He did note that the township that today contains most of the wildlife area had fewer residents and more railroad land for sale in 1902 than anyplace else in Burnett County. He advised potential buyers of the sandy land: "Farm it well and farm fewer acres than you would of clay and you will make money."

For a brief time, promoters encouraged sheep raising and goat herding, partly on the somewhat dubious theory that the animals would feed on brush and help clear the land. Overall, the promotion for the logged area of northern Wisconsin was "gaudy, simple and sentimental," according to histo-

Railroad Lands

Special attention is called to the lands of the Chicago, St. Paul, Minneapolis & Omaha Railway Company, diagrams of which are found on Pages 109 to 117. The policy of the company will be liberal to actual settlers on these lands. Sales will be made when desired on terms of one-fifth cash, balance to be paid in four annual installments with interest on the deferred payments at the rate of seven per-cent per annum, if payments are made promptly when due. The Company gives its customers the privilege of paying deferred payments on land contracts at any time and only charges interest from the contract to the date of payment.

For several years past, the Traffic Department of the Company has authorized reduced rates to land-seekers to stations in Wisconsin near which the land is located. These rates, however, are subject to change at any time without notice.

Very low rates are also made on settlers' effects or emigrants' movables and reduced rates will be made for families of settlers on application to the General Passenger Agent, St. Paul, Minn.

Parties desiring cheap farming lands that will rapidly increase in value when improved, should look over these diagrams and make an early selection.

Send all applications to G. W. Bell, Land Commissioner, Hudson, Wisconsin.

G. W. Bell, Land Commissioner,
HUDSON, WISCONSIN.

Issued as a Supplement to The Journal of Burnett County, Dec. 19, 1902.

A 1902 ad in the *Journal of Burnett County* touted cheap farm land that would "rapidly increase in value when improved." JOURNAL OF BURNETT COUNTY, 1902

rian Lucile Kane. And clearly the optimism of land promoters overshot the mark in the barrens. Once farmers arrived at their land, clearing was hard. Stump pullers and dynamite were expensive, Kane noted, and many farmers pleaded with land companies for delays in payments or for advances to help pay taxes.

But in the first two decades of the twentieth century, it seems, optimism was plentiful. Dozens of families came to the sandy soil of eastern Blaine Township in Burnett County, and for a while, a new community breathed life into the area.

By 1903, they were burying their dead in tiny Evergreen Cemetery on Five Mile Road. Three years later, children were attending Forest Home School, the eight-grade school on St. Croix Trail that you have been staking out. In 1907, just across the Washburn County line, a post office opened in a general store run by David and Dora Brewer. The post office was named "Five Mile," apparently for the nearby creek that was about five miles long, and if you asked these barrens residents where they lived, they were likely to have answered "Five Mile." The Brewers' store was a hive of activity. Residents picked up mail and brought blueberries to sell. One day, according to an old-timer quoted in an oral history of the area, a young man came in and, in the process of robbing the store, shot David Brewer's eye out.

Residents voted on everything from raising bonds for a bridge over the St. Croix River to who should be president of the United States. They leaned Republican in state and national elections (preferring Charles Hughes to Woodrow Wilson in 1916, for example). But a smattering cast ballots in 1918 for Victor Berger, a Socialist Milwaukee congressman running for the US Senate. In 1912, the men of Blaine voted 12–6 in favor of a Wisconsin referendum to give women the right to vote even as the state overwhelmingly defeated the measure by a 2–1 margin.

Farm prices were good and agriculture in northern Wisconsin was moderately successful through the teens. But despite the verve, the community ran out of gas fairly quickly. In 1917, a Burnett County highway commissioner discouraged the state from building a new highway through the area, calling the northern part of the county "all swamps and red sand." Soil that might have produced one or two good crops soon failed. The agricultural optimists of the 1890s had failed to anticipate or mention the sand's lack of nutrients and the harsh realities of the landscape. And after World War I, farm prices fell.

You can almost hear the place sighing as residents leave and local services shut their doors. The post office serving the area from the general store closed in 1919 and mail service moved to Minong fifteen miles away. The Forest Home School kept going into the 1930s, even getting replaced after it burned down, but it finally closed in 1938 as the last residents left.

6

THOSE WHO CAME TO FARM

Who were the hardscrabble folk who came to farm? Writing in the 1950s, historian Lucile Kane noted that little had been published about the immigrants who "came off rented farms, out of the factories, back from the West and over from Europe to try their hands as freeholders in Wisconsin's northland."

In 1910, about one hundred people—maybe two dozen families—lived on and next to the ten square miles that are now the Namekagon Barrens Wildlife Area in the northernmost corner of Burnett County. Land that today is empty of people was briefly a polyglot community. Half the residents were children. A third of the adults were immigrants from Scandinavia, Germany, Canada, England, and Ireland. The rest hailed from Illinois, Michigan, Iowa, Minnesota, Nebraska, Indiana, New York, and elsewhere in Wisconsin. Seven were Ojibwe, living at Dogtown on the land of their ancestors.

If you walked down St. Croix Trail (then called Minong Road) for a mile or two from the schoolhouse, you passed residents born in Germany, Denmark, Sweden, and Norway, not to mention Iowa. Sisters Mildred and Dorothy Zach, originally from Iowa, reminisced years later about visiting and picking berries with Dogtown residents and listening in the night to the drums and singing of summer ceremonies. They were thrilled; their mother was terrified, they reported.

The farm families put up temporary tarpaper shacks and then built log homes. Walls were insulated with newspapers. They cleared land with horses and, later, dynamite, and they built concrete silos and cut wild hay and raised cows, sheep, and chickens. They planted potatoes and corn and

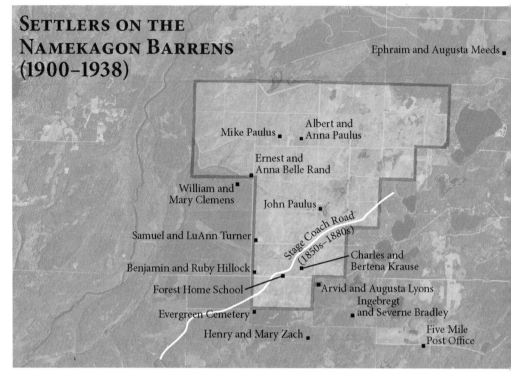

SETTLERS ON THE NAMEKAGON BARRENS (1900–1938)

Ephraim and Augusta Meeds

Mike Paulus

Albert and
Anna Paulus

Ernest and
Anna Belle Rand

William and
Mary Clemens

John Paulus

Samuel and LuAnn Turner

Stage Coach Road
(1850s–1880s)

Benjamin and Ruby Hillock

Charles and
Bertena Krause

Forest Home School

Arvid and Augusta Lyons
Ingebregt
and Severne Bradley

Evergreen Cemetery

Henry and Mary Zach

Five Mile
Post Office

MAPPING SPECIALISTS, LTD.

oats. Men frequently earned money in logging camps to supplement their families' livelihoods. They had no electricity, of course, and no indoor plumbing. These families traveled their new roads of sand by horse or on foot. A woman named Grace House served as a community doctor and midwife for people who were hours by horse and wagon from a licensed physician.

In the bare testimony of census reports, land records, and other material, you can conjure up the hopes and heartbreaks of some of these barrens men and women, people seeking to improve their lot in life or left with no other choice. Perhaps, as the Minnesota writer Bill Holm once said about his (and my) hometown on the prairie, no one came to the barrens after succeeding somewhere else. These were people on their second and third chance, and mostly they didn't prosper, at least not very long. Descendants today seem to know little of their barrens ancestors or what life held for them. Perhaps tough times were deemed better forgotten.

They had put their shoulders to the burden in front of them and then they left, weaving themselves into the American fabric elsewhere, perhaps taking along some remnant of character born on the barrens.

THE HILLOCKS

Take the Hillock family, for example. Collectively, they briefly owned more land here than anybody else.

Look around from the concrete foundation of the schoolhouse, likely attended by the children of Benjamin and Ruby Hillock. (It was known to some as Hillock School.) Walk down the sandy road to the west, pass a small stand of jack pines, and eventually you come to a depression in the brush, about thirty feet by twenty, maybe six or eight feet deep. Boulders mark what could have been a foundation; metal cans and a teapot lie rusting at the bottom, put there who knows when in the past century. This, where you might see the remains of a wolf-killed deer on a winter's day, is at least roughly where the family lived.

A depression near St. Croix Trail is all that remains of the Benjamin and Ruby Hillock farm from the early 1900s.

The Hillock family was ambitious. Humphrey Hillock was born in 1836 in Michigan and moved as a young man to Webster City, Iowa. He arrived just in time to join a militia formed in 1857 in response to an attack by a group of Santee Sioux (Dakota) during a harsh winter at the northwest Iowa community of Spirit Lake. Over the years, he served as county commissioner and sheriff. He ran a meat market and operated a farm in nearby Rose Grove, Iowa. Then in his mid-sixties, in 1901 and 1902, Humphrey agreed to pay the Chicago, St. Paul, Minneapolis & Omaha Railway more than $4,000 for about 1,600 acres some three hundred miles north of his home, most of it in the heart of what are now the sands of the wildlife area.

The railroad was known as the "Omaha Road" and later became part of the Chicago & Northwestern. The federal government had provided to a predecessor railroad (the North Wisconsin Railway) hundreds of thousands of acres of northern Wisconsin as an incentive for building a railroad from the St. Croix River to Superior and Bayfield. The resale to Hillock was one of a number of land sales the railroad made over the following decades. It's not clear why Humphrey Hillock bought the land, and little evidence exists that he did anything with it before he died in Iowa in 1911. His death was front-page news in the *Webster City Freeman*, which called him "one of the pioneer settlers of Hamilton County" and "a good man and an exemplary citizen."

If he bought the land as an investment, no records show that he resold it to make a profit. Apparently by 1903, he donated three acres for the community's Evergreen Cemetery just south of Five Mile Road. In 1912, his widow, Jennie, deeded the Hillock land over to their daughter, Grace Hillock. Grace, too, seems not to have taken an active role with the land. An absentee owner, she lived in Iowa, a teacher and a bookkeeper and a frequent subject in the social columns of the *Webster City Freeman*. The newspaper noted various social gatherings she attended or hosted and travels she made, including a visit to Wisconsin to see her brother Benjamin.

Then in 1917, Grace and her mother moved to Seattle, where another, much younger, brother, Hugh Royden Hillock, lived. She lived out her life there. A descendant of that brother knows of Grace but had never heard that she once owned more than one thousand acres of Wisconsin land. It all went to the county for failure to pay taxes in 1929.

The Hillock family was prominent in the early settlement on the barrens. Humphrey, left, bought land from the railroad and passed it on to his daughter, Grace, right. Unlike either of them, Humphrey's son Benjamin and his wife, Ruby, actually farmed for a time on the barrens. PHOTOS COURTESY OF DAVID HILLOCK

Meanwhile, son Benjamin homesteaded 160 acres and bought an additional parcel from the Omaha Road. His wife, Ruby, daughter of neighbors Joseph and Mary Gage from Walworth, Wisconsin, homesteaded another 160 acres under her own name. But then they bailed out of the barrens. Roughly fifteen years after arriving in northwestern Wisconsin, they were in Missouri, having sold their land to another Missourian who may or may not have ever gotten to the barrens.

One of their grandchildren, Virgil, says he was familiar with the family's time living on the barrens. By 1930, the family was established near Clovis, New Mexico. Ruby died of pneumonia before Virgil was born, but he had been told of her prowess as a teacher who could speak French, German, and Spanish. Approaching eighty, Virgil recalled that Benjamin lived with Virgil's family until 1953. Another descendant became the mayor of Little Elm, Texas.

ARVID AND AUGUSTA LYONS

Now walk the other way from the schoolhouse, a half mile east on St. Croix Trail to Gomulak Fire Lane, a narrow north-south strip of sand. You're at the homestead of one of the most intriguing, mysterious, and tragic barrens families: that of Arvid and Augusta Lyons.

Arvid was originally Arvid Jansson, born in Sweden in 1841. He immigrated to America at twenty-eight. It's not clear where he spent the next twenty-one years, but in 1890, he returned to Sweden and married the much younger Augusta Andersdottir. Almost as fast as humanly possible, they proceeded to have ten children. Then in 1903—he was sixty-one and she was forty-three—the family packed up and moved again, to the United States. A manifest on the ship that brought them to New York in August that year recorded that Arvid Jansson was going to join a friend in Portales, New Mexico, a "Mr. Lendsey."

It's not certain who that was (although a man named Washington Ellsworth Lindsey was about to become the mayor of Portales and eventually the governor of New Mexico). It's also not clear how Arvid Jansson came to know him or why he wanted to go to New Mexico. Portales at the time was a nascent farm community near Clovis. (Was it a coincidence that Benjamin Hillock later wound up in Clovis, an intended destination talked up by his barrens neighbor? It's impossible to know.)

Arvid seems not to have made it to the Southwest. Perhaps he saw a railroad promotion or maybe a flyer written up by Ed Peet bragging about land in Burnett County. At any rate, Arvid and Augusta next show up in the record homesteading in the barrens, taking up the federal government offer of 160 acres free and clear if you lived on it for five years. They now had the last name Lyons. A 1905 Wisconsin census shows them and their now eleven children living in Blaine Township. The first names and birth dates match precisely the Swedish church records and the ship records for the Jansson family. Arvid was listed as sixty-three; Augusta was forty-five; and the farm they homesteaded lay just west of Richart Lake. Descendants today say they were aware the family changed its name but didn't know

A stamped metal plate for Arvid Lyons is one of the few markers in Evergreen Cemetery.

why and thought, in fact, that the original name in Sweden had been Johnson.

Then, apparently, tragedy hit.

The first clue comes from the records of the Evergreen Cemetery about a mile from their farm. Four-year-old Ruth Lyons was buried in April 1906 after she "died in a bonfire," according to death records. It seems possible that the same fire took the life of Augusta, the child's mother. For one thing, by 1910 the census listed Arvid as a widower. For another, a granddaughter of the couple's son Ernest recalls today that "Grandpa Ernie always said his mother died in a fire." Whatever the details, her death apparently tore apart the family.

In the 1910 census, five of the Lyons children were listed as "foundlings" who were living with neighbors. Then in May 1914, Arvid Lyons, at seventy-three, transferred his 160 acres to his oldest daughter, Anna, and a few days later died of stomach cancer. His remains were placed in the nearby cemetery, where the metal marker bearing his name is one of only two still legible today.

The Lyons children grew up and dispersed to Milwaukee, Minnesota, and California. Son Ernest, after living with neighbors, went to work on the Soo Line and married a tavern owner in Stevens Point, where his descendants live today. Another son, Axel, moved to Waterville, Minnesota, married, and had a son he named after his father. This younger Arvid Lyons joined the US Navy at the end of World War II and served for thirty years, ending his career as a lieutenant commander and dying in the San Diego area in 2011.

Descendants today say they know little of the Lyons children and their years on the barrens. The younger Arvid Lyons "never talked about his family," his daughter reported. Did they attend the new school less than a mile from their home? Did they go blueberry picking with neighbors? Was a childhood on the barrens largely something to be forgotten? More questions remain than answers.

By 1916, the Lyons land had been taken by the county for delinquent taxes, and today it is the location of a small 1960s concrete-block hunting cabin and a picnic shelter used by the Friends of the Namekagon Barrens Wildlife Area and other groups interested in the barrens. You can't help but look around the little clearing, listening for shouting children and wondering about the fire that apparently took two lives.

CHARLES AND BERTENA KRAUSE

Step back a short distance across the intersection of St. Croix Trail and Gomulak Fire Lane and you're on land homesteaded by a young couple from Milwaukee, the Krauses. Charles immigrated as a baby in 1877, living with his family in a neighborhood of fellow Prussians in the middle of Milwaukee. His father worked as a laborer in the growing city, and by the time he was twenty-five, Charles had a job in a stove works.

He met a young Danish woman, Bertena Christensen, who had also immigrated with her family to Milwaukee. They married in 1899 and quickly headed for the barrens. Their son, Hubert, was born in 1909 or 1910 (perhaps with the help of community midwife Grace House) and they completed the process of obtaining their 160-acre farm in 1913. For a brief moment, the intersection of Gomulak and St. Croix Trail was a tiny jumble of northern Europeans: Germans, Swedes, and a Dane, with Norwegians

A few concrete blocks are all that remain of what was likely the home of Charles and Bertena Krause (*left*), who homesteaded in 1913 near what is now Gomulak Fire Lane. Pieces of broken crockery lie scattered on the Krause's land nearby (*right*).

just down the road. Yet almost immediately, the Krauses sold the land to a man in Madison—it quickly wound up in the hands of a real estate agent there—and moved back to Milwaukee, where Charles lived out his days as a farmer, dying in 1941.

No public records exist showing that anyone farmed the land after the Krauses left, although it's possible the real estate agent in Madison rented it out. Today, if you wander off Gomulak Fire Lane a little ways, you can find a clearing, some depressions that might be from a house or outbuildings, a few chunks of foundation concrete, and some broken pieces of crockery. There are even a few spears of asparagus growing, perhaps a lasting memory of the young couple.

Add another mystery to the barrens: Did the Krauses witness the fire that killed two members of the Lyons family across the road? Did they consider taking in one of the Lyons children like other neighbors did?

WILLIAM AND MARY CLEMENS

If you drive up Dry Landing Road from its intersection with St. Croix Trail for a mile and a half or so, a two-track path plunges you into the county forest to the west. That will carry you about three-tenths of a mile to a grass clearing a couple hundred feet across amid jack pines and Hill's oaks. The clearing is just south of a small creek, a short drainage flowing west out of the Namekagon Barrens and toward the St. Croix River two miles away. The main features in the clearing are two round, poured-concrete foundations about ten feet across, at one time the bases of silos for hay but now filled with growing trees. No obvious house foundation is visible, though you can spot the remains of a well.

This was the homestead of William and Mary Clemens just after 1900, a farm that seems to have been one of the more prosperous ones on the barrens. William Clemens was born around 1870 in Geneva, Iowa, to parents who had come from Pennsylvania. Geneva is close to Webster City in Hamilton County, where the Hillocks and a couple other barrens farmers hailed from. (Were the barrens getting talked up among the adventurous of Hamilton County? Was there a connection to the fact that the Omaha Road ran near there?)

Around 1902, William married sixteen-year-old Mary, whose parents were Bohemian and had come from Nebraska. The couple apparently arrived on the barrens around 1905, raising hogs, cattle, and chickens. They registered their 160-acre homestead with the federal land office in 1913. The 1915 Burnett County plat book lists their postal address as Five Mile, and in 1920, they had a boarder, a schoolteacher named Anna McGrew. By 1923, the farm had expanded to 240 acres, and the Clemenses were among the very few farmers in the area with two silos, according to a federal farm enumeration. The couple also owned a purebred bull.

A year later, though, they and their three children—Alfred, James R., and Edith—were gone from the barrens. By the late 1920s their land, like so much around it, had reverted to the county for back taxes. At some point, the creek running south of their land came to be named for the family. The more or less parallel creek running on the north side of their property became Rand Creek because it passed the small neighboring farms of three members of the Rand family. Not far downstream, the creeks run together and on to the St. Croix River.

The Clemens family wound up in Cumberland, Wisconsin, about sixty miles south, where son Alfred apparently died in 1923. They later moved to Hennepin County in Minnesota, where William farmed, Mary worked as a mender in a laundry, and son James was a filling station attendant. Perhaps the family moved back to Cumberland; when they died—William in 1947, James in 1953, and Mary in 1961—all were buried in Lakeside Cemetery in Cumberland. The record for daughter Edith is scant, but perhaps her hand can be seen on Mary's 1961 tombstone, inscribed simply "Mother."

INGEBREGT AND SEVERNE BRADLEY

Each May, three lavender lilacs still bloom close to a low foundation wall that was a home one hundred years ago. Just southwest of Bradley Lake near the Washburn-Burnett county line, the lilacs, hemmed in by the young forest around them, are another reminder of the human endeavor on the barrens.

A good size, thirty-six by thirty-six feet, the square foundation walls were poured concrete about eight inches across, containing stone, bricks, and other fill. The walls are mostly gone, but smaller depressions nearby mark the location of outhouses, perhaps, or storage sheds. Across a clearing, two other foundations remain. Concrete marks the rectangular foundation of what was perhaps a barn, and a circle of concrete is the remains of a silo, about twelve feet across.

This was the residence on 160 acres homesteaded by Ingebregt T. and Severne Bradley just after 1900. Ingebregt (spelled Engebregt in some records) was born in Norway in 1854 and came to America at eighteen. Severne (spelled Severene and Severena in some records) was born in Minnesota in 1868. The couple married in Albert Lea, Minnesota, in 1887 and came to this land around 1904. In the 1910 census, they were listed with six children, four still living with them, ages three to seventeen.

Ten years later, the couple was still there but only a granddaughter lived with them. By this time, Ingebregt was sixty-six and Severne was fifty-two. Records are incomplete but it seems possible that three of their

Lilacs bloom every spring on the former homestead of the Bradleys.

children, daughters Carolyne and Stella and son Severt, lie buried a mile west in Evergreen Cemetery.

The family farmed until 1929, growing corn, hay, and soybeans and keeping chickens and pigs. Ingebregt died, and Severne was listed in census records as a widow in 1930. The farm, which today lies on county land just outside the boundaries of the state wildlife area, went for back taxes by 1936.

But the lilacs still bloom.

Henry and Mary Zach

In 1917, the Zachs arrived with a flourish. Living in Sioux City, Iowa, Henry and Mary Zach bought forty acres from the railroad for $240 and came to Minong by train.

According to daughters Mildred and Dorothy, they boarded a lumber wagon driven by a woman who wound up racing an alcohol-fueled neighbor: "I can still see and hear the wagons bumping along—horses galloping and whips flying—trunks, bundles and children bouncing around together, with Mother hanging onto her hat and screaming bloody murder. She was scared to death but we girls enjoyed it much," the Zach sisters wrote years later. With that, the family built a log house and settled in, growing corn, potatoes, and beans, according to the 1923 farm census. Eventually they raised chickens and even planted fruit trees.

"Our entertainment was house parties," wrote Mildred and Dorothy Zach in 1968. Looking back on these times, the Zach sisters explained that "babies were put to bed and young and old alike danced until daylight. Sometimes we were lucky enough to have violin and guitar; otherwise, we wound up the phonograph and danced the night through. In the winter months we popped corn and made candy. The house parties were more frequent during the summer months, as there were no snowplowed roads in those days. We looked forward each spring to the first house party."

The Zachs arrived later than many and stayed longer than most. The family held onto the farm until the government bought them out in 1938. Then they moved south to Oakland, near Webster, where Henry farmed and worked for creameries in the area and died in 1963. By that time, daughter Mildred had married a man named Fred Anderson, who had grown up not far from her family near the Five Mile store. (Fred Anderson was, in fact, a brother to five children who lie buried in the Evergreen Cemetery under a marker that says—barely legible now—"Anderson babies.")

Another Zach son born on the barrens, Henry Roy, fought in World War II and was wounded during the Battle of the Bulge in December 1944, one of few American soldiers to survive what became known as the Malmedy massacre.

THE PAULUS FAMILY

The Paulus family was another set of wanderers who came to the barrens, stayed a decade or so, and then moved on.

Albert and Anna Paulus were in their fifties when they arrived. After immigrating from Luxembourg as children, they had married in Nebraska and lived for a decade in St. Paul. Their large family included twin sons John and Michael. They tried farming in western Minnesota for a few years and then decided to come to the barrens to homestead. By 1910, the family had three homesteads of 160 acres each on the barrens. Albert and Anna held one farm and John and Michael each had another.

If you wander the scrub oak and aspen of those farms today, you can still detect grassy areas where fields were once cleared, and here and there are a few depressions in the sand that mark the locations of buildings. But by 1920, the Pauluses were gone from the barrens. They appear in the federal census in western Minnesota again, Traverse County this time. No longer with farms of their own, John and Mike were living with their parents, "working out" as hired laborers to other farmers. They moved again in the 1920s, winding up in Aitkin County in Minnesota by 1930. By then Albert and Anna were living with John on a farm. Albert died that year; Anna lived until 1942. Daughter Isabel, who had been born in 1886 in St. Paul, stayed in the area after her family left, living out her years in nearby Gordon.

THE TURNERS AND THE RANDS

Families on the barrens were sometimes multigenerational and intermarried affairs; this was the case for the Turners and the Rands. Samuel Turner was born in 1861 in southern Wisconsin, and before he was a year old, his father, Thomas, joined the First Wisconsin Cavalry and went off to fight in the Civil War. The regiment saw action and suffered casualties in the campaign to capture Atlanta, but Thomas returned home to farm and eventually moved his family north to central Wisconsin.

At twenty-seven, Samuel married LuAnn Bailey, a Pierce County resident just shy of her fourteenth birthday. They had a daughter, Anna Belle, in 1890, the first of nine children. For a time, Samuel supported them as a laborer, but then, when he was in his mid-forties, they moved farther north to farm. First, Samuel, LuAnn, and six children rented a farm near Minong in Washburn County, east of the barrens.

Daughter Anna Belle then married Ernest Rand and moved to the barrens, homesteading on Dry Landing Road next to Ernest's father, Simeon, and brother, Bert. The Rands had come from New York. Then Anna Belle's parents made it a real family affair, also settling on the barrens. By 1915, Samuel and LuAnn Turner were homesteading just down the road from the Rand farms and adding to their family. Their youngest, Clifford, was born in 1913.

The Turners stayed put on their 160 acres longer than most, until at least 1931. They raised chickens, grew potatoes and corn, and planted plum trees. Two sons registered for the draft in 1918, listing their home as Five Mile, the post office across the county line in Washburn County. Samuel Turner voted regularly in Blaine Township, and he typically listed his address as Five Mile, even in 1926, some years after the Five Mile post office had closed. The 1930 census listed the family alongside their nearby neighbors the Zachs and the Bradleys, but few others.

"I know they had a pretty rough life," said Beatrice Roatch, a great-granddaughter still living in the region. "They were poor, very poor." But the evidence of their hard work is still there. You can see the path of the driveway leading to a depression in the brush prairie left by the Turners' home. There's a five-foot-long foundation wall where you can find broken glass, dishes, and crockery, possibly once belonging to the family. Retired DNR wildlife technician Gary Dunsmoor remembers finding a page from a 1936 newspaper at the site, apparently used as insulation and later dug out by a badger. The plum trees bore fruit well into the twenty-first century.

Samuel died in 1949, after moving to Siren. Two years later, LuAnn died. A number of descendants live in western Wisconsin and east-central Minnesota.

THE MEEDS FAMILY

Perhaps no one illustrates the second-chance nature of barrens farmers as well as the family of Ephraim Emery Meeds and Augusta Meeds. Augusta emigrated from Germany at eight with her grandparents; Ephraim was the son of a man who died in the Civil War. The couple and their children came to the barrens in 1916 after a number of medical and other setbacks forced them to sell their home and belongings in Menomonie. Ephraim (who went by Emery) was fifty-three and Augusta was thirty-seven.

The couple moved onto land that had been homesteaded by others but then given up, just north of the Washburn-Douglas county line, about two miles from what is now the wildlife area. They moved into the log home previous owners had built and made it work for a short time, cutting wild hay and feeding cows. Years later, Jennie Meeds Terry, their daughter, remembered the cold weather, walking a mile to school, how the family horses died of disease, how they only once had a Christmas tree. The kids slept two or three to a bed with ticks of cornhusks or hay. When a neighbor girl died one winter, the girl's brother skied some fifteen miles to Minong to get material for Jennie's father to build a casket.

Ephraim and Augusta Meeds came to the barrens in 1916 after suffering reversals of fortune elsewhere. Their daughter Jennie later wrote a short reminiscence, recalling times both hard and pleasant. PHOTO COURTESY CAROL SMITH

From left, Elsie, Jennie, Ella, and Anne Meeds, children raised on the barrens. PHOTO COURTESY CAROL SMITH

Jennie also recalled the fear of nearby forest fires, remembering vividly the October 12, 1918, Cloquet fire and the strong smell of smoke. One year, her father grew a good crop of oats only to have the wind and sand destroy it. "The sand cut the oats off slick and clean," she wrote. "I remember the sun would look like a big red ball and the cows would stay in the barnyard and bellow and bellow . . . a real eerie feeling." At one point, the family's two horses died so they rode their neighbor's blind-in-one-eye pony to Five Mile.

Twice, Jennie remembered fondly, she spent the summer in a tent at Dairyland, a small town ten miles from home, helping her dad cut hay with a scythe and stack it for the family cows. To be sure, she also remembered with fondness the wildflowers she came across while out caring for her family's cows, the family garden, dances at school, the pigs they raised every year and butchered in the fall. She learned self-sufficiency, perhaps mainly from her strong-willed German immigrant mother. But in the end the barrens claimed their livelihood, too, and the couple and Jennie all lived out their lives in nearby Gordon.

THE LAST ONES LEAVE

The federal census of 1920 showed a barrens population about a third the size it had been ten years earlier. Arvid and Augusta Lyons were dead; the Hillocks had left; and the Paulus family was back in Minnesota, looking for a third and fourth chance. Alfred S. Keating, a middle-aged bachelor from England, had farmed 240 acres right on the old stagecoach road where it passed into Washburn County. He left, however, and died of liver cancer in Sheridan, Wyoming.

Carl and Marie Eckert had come from South Dakota with four young children and Marie's parents. Each couple filed for a 160-acre homestead around 1906 just north of the old stagecoach road. The Eckerts added a half dozen children to their family (one of whom would be killed in action in 1945 after crossing the Roer River in Germany with the US Army), but within a few years they moved back west, to Rugby, North Dakota.

The promise of agriculture, held out by promoters and academics alike, had proved fickle. By the late teens and into the 1920s and 1930s, farmers tried to sell out, and parcels sometimes turned over every year or two.

A spring full moon rises behind a solitary jack pine on a barrens land now empty of residents.

Often the land simply was taken by Burnett County when owners stopped paying property taxes. For a while, the county would resell the land to new owners, but eventually even that practice faded.

The Keating property on the county line is a good example of the high turnover rate. In 1916, Keating moved west to Wyoming, sold his farm to a family member who was a doctor in Sheridan, and died within weeks. The family member, Vincent Keating, and his wife, Claire, sold the land the next year to another Sheridan couple. In 1921, a couple from Minnesota bought it and then promptly sold it to a man from Los Angeles. Two years later, he sold it to a couple from the Stillwater, Minnesota, area. They then sold it to a couple from Blue Earth County, Minnesota. It's not clear what the motivation was for all of these purchases or whether any of the new owners showed up. But finally Burnett County claimed it for delinquent property taxes in 1927.

In the vault of the register of deeds in Siren, Wisconsin, a verdict about the former Keating farm fairly jumps off the yellowing pages of a leather-bound volume. In 1932, the county included the farm in a long list of properties to be designated under the state's new forest crop law. The land, the county declared, was "more useful for growing timber and other forest crops than for any other purpose."

When geographer Raymond E. Murphy surveyed the region in 1930, he found its children "grown up and gone." No new people were coming in. Dairy herds were poorly fed, he reported, and many homes were tumbled down. Furthermore, he noted, "the limited fertility of the sandy soil has been exhausted by continuous cropping with little rotation or fertilization, and many farms have been abandoned and allowed to revert to barrens or forest."

The Northern Wisconsin Settler Relocation Project made final the ending of the era. Starting in 1934, the program used federal dollars to pay farm families to move off unproductive land and find a better life elsewhere. Those who never left died from a litany of causes: childbirth, scarlet fever, diphtheria, tuberculosis, pneumonia, heart problems. One suicide was noted in county death records. Despite the sense of community, the parties and sleigh rides, romances and flower-gathering excursions, it's hard to find someone from this era who was born there, grew up, made a living, and lived to a ripe old age on the Namekagon Barrens.

"Here we have some of the best examples in the nation of misguided settlement," University of Minnesota professor R. I. Nowell concluded in 1937, a year and a half after he took over directing the federal resettlement effort in Wisconsin, Minnesota, and Michigan. In less than a lifetime, the barrens had proved unable to support American agriculture. It's tempting to conclude these people of the barrens were wanderers more than they were sedentary, perhaps by choice, perhaps by necessity.

Many years later, asked why his great grandfather left the barrens for Missouri in 1917, Oklahoma resident Virgil Hillock said, "It was too dang cold," a simple explanation that perhaps was not the whole reason. For some, at least, the barrens never stopped being a place of enchantment. Decades after they moved from the barrens, the Zach sisters concluded their joint reminiscence with the words, "It is still paradise."

7

A Choice

It's August 12, 1938. The Turners, the Rands, and even the Zachs have left. John Kenebec, the last Ojibwe Dogtown resident, has died. But the Namekagon Barrens are not quiet today. If you stand at your spot by the Forest Home School—the building still upright but finally closed—you'll hear the thrum of an airplane overhead, flying one way, then the other. Back and forth.

More than eighty years after Hiram Fellows dragged his heavy surveying equipment past, the government is surveying again, this time using the infant technology of aerial photography. Intent on reducing surpluses to keep farm prices high and providing incentives for soil conservation, the administration of Franklin D. Roosevelt wanted to track what farmers were doing with their cropland. The administration started experimenting with aerial photography by 1934, and within a year or two it was taking photographs of hundreds of thousands of square miles, including areas in northern Wisconsin. Field and support crews went to great lengths to determine scale and precise locations, and photographs were overlapped to provide stereo images.

The black-and-white photos of the barrens, squares roughly three miles on a side, are remarkable, freezing a moment just as a new controversy was warming over what to do with the region. You can make out the rectangles and trapezoids of farm fields that Benjamin Hillock, Albert Paulus, and others scratched out, cleared, and then left behind. You can spot the path the Zach children once walked to school. William Clemens's two silos still stand in the photos. A ravine that is Clemens Creek gradually

You can see in this 1938 aerial photo the light-colored fields left behind by homesteading farmers. St. Croix Trail runs east-west through the middle of the photo, and in the center you can make out the small rectangle around the Forest Home School. STATE CARTOGRAPHER'S OFFICE, UNIVERSITY OF WISCONSIN–MADISON

widens to the west before it joins the St. Croix River. The old stagecoach road cuts a fading diagonal toward the northeast.

It's noticeable how little of the barrens appears to actually have been farmed. In any given 640-acre section, maybe a hundred acres or fewer show signs of being cleared. The land Humphrey Hillock bought from the railroad in 1901 and 1902 appears in the aerials to be wide open and mostly unplowed. Clumps of trees appear, but the land is mostly sparse brush, perhaps the same scrub oaks that still pepper the landscape today.

Farm censuses of the 1920s and 1930s confirm this impression. Although the barrens farmers may have homesteaded or bought 160 acres, the land they actually farmed for potatoes or hay or corn amounted to maybe ten or twenty acres. Clearing and plowing had been hard work. Scanning your eyes over the photos is like looking for ghosts.

But the farmers were gone and farming on the barrens was done. By 1928, Dean Harry Russell had declared the land of northern Wisconsin mostly unsuitable for farming, a stunning reversal by the University of Wisconsin's College of Agriculture. A different inventory of Wisconsin's land at about the same time, known as the Bordner Survey for its director John Bordner, mapped the area in detail. It confirms what the aerial photos show. Around your schoolhouse spot, there's nothing noted but scrub oak and jack pine less than six inches in diameter. What these aerial photos don't show you is that a fight was about to break out on this now lonely land.

For those contemplating how the land should be used, the first impulse was to look to trees. Only thirty years after pleading for immigrants to farm Wisconsin's north, the state turned back to forestry. Counties like Burnett were saddled with thousands of acres of tax-delinquent property. Desperate for a way to make the land productive and under pressure to help these counties, the state created incentives to grow and harvest timber.

In 1927, the state legislature enacted a law that gave owners a property tax break if they managed their land to maximize timber harvesting. Counties were soon allowed to include their recently acquired tax-delinquent lands in the effort. So in 1932, Burnett County began "enrolling" its former farmland under the forest crop law, a law still in effect today. The state provides the county with technical assistance and loans that can be paid back when the county sells the timber. The result

A tree-planting crew works in the Chequamegon-Nicolet National Forest in 1935. WHI IMAGE ID 6375

was—and still is—millions of dollars in revenue for Burnett and other counties across Wisconsin.

The county planted hundreds of acres of trees, sometimes with the help of the federal Civilian Conservation Corps, armies of young men and women who were recruited to take on a variety of building and growing projects throughout the nation during the Depression. A few remnants of one CCC camp still stand just a few miles south of the wildlife area. Suppression of fire—the very thing that made the barrens what they were for thousands of years—became an important goal of state forestry efforts. Smokey Bear was about to arrive on the scene.

But not everyone thought this emphasis on forestry was such a good idea.

In the fall of 1935, Frederick and Frances Hamerstrom, a young couple from the East Coast, rolled into Necedah, Wisconsin, in a tan Essex roadster

Frances and Frederick Hamerstrom, shown here with their mentor, Aldo Leopold, were instrumental in turning attention to wildlife habitat management instead of forestry. ELVA PAULSON

piled high with boxes and furniture. Frederick had come to work for
Roosevelt's Resettlement Administration, helping farmers move off land
that was unproductive for farming and turning it instead into reserves
for game. The Hamerstroms were inspired by Aldo Leopold, the Wisconsin conservationist credited with fostering the environmental ethic of
the twentieth century. The couple would spend most of the rest of their
lives studying and trying to preserve the brush prairie and barrens habitats they and many others could see were rapidly disappearing from
Wisconsin.

In central Wisconsin, near the towns of Necedah and Black River
Falls, the resettlement program worked to dam drainage ditches, restore
marshes, and improve trout streams. The couple set about mapping and
measuring the area's wildlife—prairie chickens, sharp-tailed grouse, sandhill cranes, white-tailed deer, and more. They trapped and banded and
established experimental food plots; they found nest sites and mating
dance grounds; they collected hundreds of plants. The Hamerstroms eventually grew disillusioned with the bureaucracy of the Resettlement Administration, but they built on what they had learned, joining Leopold's
new graduate program at the University of Wisconsin in Madison.

Among other things, the Hamerstroms shared with Leopold an affinity
for prairie chickens and sharp-tailed grouse. Eventually both Hamerstroms went to work for the Wisconsin Conservation Department, the
predecessor to the Department of Natural Resources.

By the 1940s, state wildlife experts understood Wisconsin was losing
its populations of these birds, once considered both plentiful and the object
of an exquisite hunting experience. The reason: their habitat was being
turned to forest, at least partly because timber brought much-needed revenue to county governments. State game biologist Wallace Grange warned
in 1948 that grouse populations were in danger. Grange, who ten years
previously had done some early experimenting with controlled fires in
central Wisconsin, was plainspoken in arguing for the value of fire in maintaining those populations:

> Wisconsin's citizens have been taught the dangers of forest fires,
> the necessity for forest covering as a water conservation aid, and
> the desirability of having vast tree growth nearly everywhere except

on actual farms. So well has this lesson been taught that many sincere conservationists have but rudimentary knowledge of the fact that if Wisconsin succeeds in reforesting all of its valuable "barrens," old fields, open northern bogs and similar openings, it thereby depreciates the whole quality of the country from the wildlife standpoint.

Ten years later, Grange's words were echoed by University of Wisconsin botanist John T. Curtis in his sweeping classic of plant ecology, *The Vegetation of Wisconsin*. Curtis wrote that grouse and blueberry harvests were threatened by the "bureaucratic dictum, that since most forest fires are the source of economic loss, therefore all fires are bad and must be prevented at any cost. This dogma has been supported by such an intensive propaganda campaign that there is danger of its being accepted as truth. On the contrary, the facts plainly indicate that fire is a normal environmental influence in the life of the forest."

Preserving the relatively open brush prairie for the birds became an important cause for the Hamerstroms and others, and in the early 1950s their

In this 1952 photo, Frederick Hamerstrom looks over an opening on the Namekagon Barrens that had been recently planted with pine trees. ELVA PAULSON

attention was drawn to the Namekagon Barrens. What had been good ground for grouse hunters was turning into pine plantations under the county forest law. Along with Oswald E. Mattson, the couple wrote a booklet published by the Conservation Department, *Sharptails into the Shadows?* They echoed Grange, mincing no words: "The openings and brushlands so necessary to the existence of sharptails are being 'crowded out' by the natural process of plant succession and by the man-made processes of plantings and fire protection." They clearly had the Namekagon Barrens in their sights, calling it one of the two or three best sharp-tailed grouse areas in northern Wisconsin. A sprawling land of open grass, blueberries, sweet fern, and scrub oak, they lamented, was planted with pine trees in April and May 1952. "Why was it not saved for sharptails? Because there is a forest crop law which offers a strong inducement to plant trees, but there is no comparable inducement to leaving openings unplanted for wildlife."

Foresters and local officials resisted, some expressing doubts the grouse could be brought back, others arguing that the revenue timber sales brought to local governments was too important. But the Hamerstroms' reputation grew, and the idea of state management of brush prairie habitat took hold. Hunting clubs and other nonprofit organizations pitched in to acquire or lease land. In 1953, the leaders of the conservation department adopted "The Wisconsin Prairie Grouse Management Policy," promoting "multiple uses for wild lands" and promising to make every effort to "maintain a huntable population through management and restoration of habitat for these birds." The policy recognized the frequent incompatibility between grouse and forestry management practices.

The debate was contentious within Burnett County. Wildlife proponents sought delays in tree-planting plans; foresters planted anyway. Finally, in 1956, a ten-year deal was struck: the county would withdraw nearly 5,700 acres from the forest crop law designation and lease it to the state at a yearly rate of twenty cents per acre. The deal created the Namekagon Barrens Wildlife Area, and wildlife managers began clearing the barrens and lighting prescribed fires. But the political tussles didn't end. The county sought to reduce the wildlife area when the lease was up in 1966. The Hamerstroms complained that state foresters were failing to cooperate. A state conservation department official voiced concern over opposition from the county board chairman.

A sharp-tailed grouse catches the morning sun in a jack pine.

In the early 1990s, the lease came up again. Complaining that the state had ignored them and treated them unfairly, county officials pressed the state for greater compensation to make up for the potential timber revenue they were forgoing. The county argued that the lease payments from the state were insufficient and it threatened to take back the entire wildlife area.

Local officials were not motivated so much by a "trees-versus-habitat" argument as by simply trying to protect taxpayers and making the land generate as much money as possible, according to Mike Luedeke, then the administrator overseeing Burnett County forests. Budget-conscious county officials believed they could get more revenue from timber than from the state's lease payments. In addition, residents in the vicinity of controlled burns complained about smoke and the perceived danger of the fires.

The DNR, the Nature Conservancy, and other groups pleaded with the county to keep the area designated as wildlife habitat, ultimately offering higher lease payments and arguing the potential timber revenue the county wanted would take a long time to materialize. At one point, realizing that some county officials knew little about the barrens, proponents led the full county board on a bus tour, getting stuck in the sand in

the process. Bruce Moss, a DNR staff specialist at the time, had organized
the tour and momentarily despaired of getting a Greyhound bus out of the
sand in the remote country. But board members got out of the bus to
lighten the load and started pushing. As Moss remembers it, the bus gradually started rolling, and the effort of accomplishing something collectively put the members in the right frame of mind to go along with a new
DNR lease. "The bus getting stuck was what sold the county board," Moss
says today.

At the end of those negotiations in 1991 and 1992, Burnett County again
signed a twenty-five-year lease but took back more than five hundred
acres, including what once had been Hillock land west of Dry Landing
Road, a chunk southeast of the Evergreen Cemetery near the Zach home,
and a "middle unit" that sat between the north and south units. The land

The wildlife area has been managed for nearly seventy years by the Wisconsin
Department of Natural Resources.

Frederick and Frances Hamerstrom dig up the root of a scrub oak on the Nameka-gon Barrens in 1952. The small tree was analyzed and found to be forty-five years old. ELVA PAULSON

taken back by the county was returned to the tree-planting program, and some of the middle unit was planted in red pine the same year.

But finally, in 2015, as the lease was again nearing its end, the state and county engineered a land swap. At about the same time, the national non-profit Conservation Fund helped purchase additional forest land from a private timber company. In the end, the now state-owned wildlife area included 6,438 acres, including some land in northwestern Washburn County. That is as much land as the wildlife area has ever included.

Today, you don't need to rely on government aerial photos to see the current state of the landscape. If you look at the ubiquitous satellite images that are refreshed regularly on the internet, you can still make out the faint outlines of a few one-hundred-year-old farm fields. But mostly you'll notice the stark difference between the dark green of the county forest that surrounds the wildlife area and the lighter hues where wildlife managers have put fire back on the land.

8

SAVING THE GROUSE

The most intriguing thing to do on the barrens is to get up in the dark on a chilly April or May morning, quietly climb into one of several viewing blinds the DNR erects, and wait for the extraordinary sharp-tailed grouse mating dance.

At dawn, two or three dozen males creep out of the brush onto open grassy areas known as leks. Soon they are pounding their feet, extending their wings, and clicking with their pointed tails in the air, displaying purple neck feathers. The noise is surprisingly loud, audible for two hundred feet or more. The males dance and turn like wind-up toys gone wild and then abruptly stop, only to begin again a minute or two later. Females watch and choose.

It's comic to humans, but it's a classic case of sexual selection. The males have evolved to engage in the display that best leads to copulation and reproductive success. By eight o'clock they're off, done with their display until the next morning. You're free to go get breakfast.

The grouse are an indicator, a flagship standing in for a complex ecosystem. More than anything else, it was to preserve these birds that the state started managing the barrens in the 1950s. A bird that once was found across the state is now limited to a few scattered places in the north. What is more, the genetic diversity of the birds has declined. Populations fluctuate, but birders estimate the state's population of males may be only in the hundreds, many of them in the Namekagon Barrens Wildlife Area.

These are actually a subspecies known as the prairie sharp-tailed grouse, which belong to one of a number of grouse species in North America. They are similar to prairie chickens. The birds weigh up to two pounds

Sharp-tailed grouse perform a flamboyant mating dance every spring on grassy clearings known as leks. MELISSA ANDERSON

and are sixteen to eighteen inches long. They have round bodies and short, rounded wings, and they lack distinctive color except for a yellow comb over each eye and, among males, a pale violet air sac on each side of the neck.

After the wild mating dance culminates, the females lay clutches of ten to fourteen eggs, incubating them for twenty-four days. Ten days after hatching, the young can fly, and in six to eight weeks they are on their own. Naturalists estimate that at one time, 13.2 percent of northern Wisconsin was covered in the open and changing habitats conducive to sharp-tailed grouse. Today that figure is less than one percent, according to the state's grouse management plan.

How, then, to encourage the rebound of sharp-tailed grouse?

The grouse thrive on "edge" terrain, seeking different cover at different times of year. They like to move back and forth seasonally from grasses to shrubs to trees, using grassy mating grounds in spring, nest areas between brush and open space in summer, and sheltering marshes in winter. Even so, DNR wildlife manager Nancy Christel says she's seen grouse out in the open brush in the winter. The birds don't migrate long distances.

Distribution of sharp-tailed
grouse has declined greatly
in Wisconsin. LARRY GREGG,
WISCONSIN DEPARTMENT OF
NATURAL RESOURCES

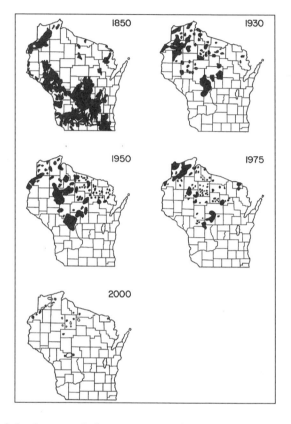

    The sharp-tailed grouse
diet varies. In winter, the
birds eat buds from birch and
aspen trees and hazelnuts. At
spring nesting time, they
turn to wintergreen berries,
green grass shoots, and the
leaves and flowers of pussy-
toes. In summer, they eat
blueberries, shrub leaves,
and grasshoppers and other
insects. In the fall, the diet
turns to grains, seeds, and
berries. They eat acorns and
rose hips in fall, winter, and
spring.

    The patchwork mosaic of the barrens is important, and the key to
creating grouse habitat, wildlife managers say, is to keep creating open
terrain by timber clearing, mechanical cutting and, mainly, fire.

    Fire on the barrens is a good example of how human and natural
history mesh. US Forest Service researchers have dated tree fire scars in
the Northwest Sands to as early as 1591. For centuries ending in the 1930s,
fire frequency in their Moquah Barrens study area in the Chequamegon-
Nicolet National Forest averaged just under thirteen years.

    But the number went up and down as the population and economic
activity changed. Fires increased for a time as the French fur trade resulted
in a greater Ojibwe population in the area. Logging, railroads, and farming
resulted in a greater intensity and number of fires. Then, after the 1930s,
fire suppression efforts pretty much eliminated wildfire in much of the
Sands. So is any given fire a natural event or a human-influenced event?
It's hard to distinguish sometimes.

The last considerable wildfire to visit what is now the wildlife area took place in 1931. It started just north of the Namekagon River and moved northeast along the St. Croix, spreading over most of what later became the wildlife area's north unit. It is recorded in state files as a "debris fire," apparently started by a farmer clearing land.

By 1953, the land that was about to became the wildlife area was a mix of red pines newly planted under the forest crop law, grass, upland brush, stands of oak and jack pines and, in the wet ravines, alder and other low-land trees. Young trees that had been recorded by the Bordner Survey and photographed in 1938 were older and larger.

Once state wildlife biologists began taking action on the barrens in the 1950s, they bulldozed abandoned farm buildings and then set about clearing timber, a process that lasted into the 1970s. In some places, they planted buckwheat and clover as grouse food sources, a practice that was later discontinued. Wildlife managers have used mowing, other cutting, and roughing up the land to keep some of the barrens open. Forest clearing has continued in newly acquired areas.

But most dramatically, they brought back fire. Fire remains a crucial tool, especially in the regeneration of grasses and flowering plants. Wildlife managers set the first controlled burn in the wildlife area in the late 1950s in the northwest corner of the north unit. That area was already open grass and brush land, which Humphrey Hillock had bought from the railroad nearly sixty years earlier and apparently never farmed or planted to pines.

The wildlife area today is carved into more than two dozen "burn units" that are on a roughly seven-year rotation. The oaks are burned ("top-killed" in the habitat specialists' lingo) and then grow back from their roots; a few tall pines are left for "structure." Grass and brush grow back quickly. A month after a burn, you see a lot of green, although a walk through the area quickly renders your pant legs sooty.

A good burn generates new grasses, sedges, and shrubs at the expense of trees. Fire essentially prunes the woody growth of food sources like blueberries, bearberries, raspberries, and others, causing them to fruit more prolifically. (One DNR veteran says he waits for the second year after a burn and then goes blueberry picking.) Among the scrub oaks, fire clears underbrush, giving grouse better access to acorns.

A Wisconsin DNR crew conducts a prescribed fire on the barrens. WISCONSIN DEPARTMENT OF NATURAL RESOURCES

As game biologist Wallace Grange pointed out in 1948, fires both destroy and create, so getting the balance right is important for the crews that conduct them. And land managers use alternatives to fire sometimes. In Douglas County to the north, they combine timber harvest and "scarifying" the ground as a way to avoid fire and still achieve the land disturbance that can be conducive to grouse use. And in Bayfield County, county foresters are trying a slightly different approach at the 11,300-acre Barnes Barrens. They use fire to keep open a core area of about a thousand acres and then plant and harvest jack pine in cycles in the areas around that core. This approach essentially uses timber clearing and some chemical control to maintain open areas.

BURNING THE BARRENS

The art of burning is the practice of maintaining a piece of land in the earliest stage of what would be its normal succession. Do nothing but put

(*Above*) A bur oak leaf collects morning dew a few days after a prescribed fire on the barrens. (*Below*) It doesn't take long after a fire for green shoots to emerge from the blackened earth.

out naturally occurring fires and eventually you have a tall pine forest. Burn it (or otherwise keep it cleared) and you have barrens.

The controlled burn season usually starts in April, some years as early as March, shortly after the winter snows have melted. Nancy Christel, longtime wildlife biologist and property manager at the Namekagon Barrens, says burn bosses vary in how they decide when a given plot of land is ready for burning. A key for her is how much aspen has grown in low areas: "I want to keep ahead of the aspen, not let it get too large." Also, hazelnut bushes and prairie willows can dominate over blueberries and sweet fern and inhibit the growth of grasses and flowers, another signal an area is ready to burn. Likewise, she wants to keep oaks and jack pines from getting too large.

Sometimes a chunk of land is ready to burn five years after the previous fire, sometimes seven. So the DNR goal at the wildlife area is to burn about one thousand acres a year. Managers try to burn the land in a patchwork, varying how hot the fires are, whether they burn in spring or fall, and burning, for example, only one of the grouse mating dance areas in a given year. Once a section is earmarked for burning, the weather watching starts.

A motion-sensitive trail camera captured a prescribed fire moving through part of the north unit in early May 2021. SNAPSHOT WISCONSIN/GARY DUNSMOOR

Relative humidity of 25 percent or less will yield a hot fire. So will higher temperatures and drier conditions in the grasses and scrub. Wind helps push a fire, but crews don't want it to go too fast.

At the wildlife area, fire crews of maybe fifteen to twenty people conduct a burn. Some are "igniters" and others are situated around the burn area to hold it in. Six to ten vehicles with water tanks stand guard around the fire. In an ideal situation, igniters start the fire on a downwind side or corner bordered by fire breaks. They let it burn slowly into the wind. After a swath is blackened, igniters move around the remaining sides of the burn unit, eventually meeting on the side opposite and upwind of the starting point. They then let the fire burn downwind toward the blackened starting point, completing the burn. Even during a "cool" fire, you can stand on the road nearby and feel the heat from flames that reach five, ten, or even more feet in the air. Smoke billows skyward, visible for miles. Fire breaks hem the fire in and crews stay until the embers are out.

A good burn, in Christel's mind, leaves the burn area about 80 percent blackened. Rejuvenation can be astonishingly quick. She has seen grouse fly back within minutes of a fire. Coyotes, fox, and raptors quickly

Three weeks later, the same camera caught five turkeys pecking for food amid the green shoots that had emerged. SNAPSHOT WISCONSIN/GARY DUNSMOOR

Spiders are among the first to get busy after a prescribed fire blackens the vegetation of the barrens.

reinvade, hunting small mammals that now are more visible. Grasses and forbs, or flowering plants, send up green shoots within days. Blueberry plants emerge in the sunlight; the insect mix changes, inviting more birds.

Oaks start growing again from the protected roots and the trunks. Jack pines are blackened but their cones open when exposed to high heat and give rise to new seedlings. Tall red pines can survive because their bark is thick, letting them stand as sentinels. Fire releases nitrogen into the soil. Ash falling to the ground provides a variety of nutrients for different plants, all varying in what they take up.

Writing in 1959 about a controlled fire in Crex Meadows two springs earlier, John T. Curtis said, "It was an exceedingly hot crown fire which totally destroyed the tops of the trees. Examination of the area in July of that year revealed over 70 prairie species, most of them in bloom or in bud." In comparison, he said, "A casual examination of unburned control

Prairie buttercups bloom early, the blossom appearing in still-blackened terrain in the April after a summer burn.

areas of identical forest revealed only a small fraction of the total list of prairie plants."

THE GROUSE

After more than sixty years of trying to preserve and boost the sharp-tailed grouse population on the barrens, how robust is it? It isn't difficult to encounter grouse on the barrens. As you walk the brush, it's fairly common to flush them from their hiding places or see them perched in treetops. In 2011, the state identified two or possibly three "metapopulations" of grouse in Wisconsin. But today only one remains: the population in the Northwest Sands. That makes the area the stronghold for the bird in Wisconsin, according to Dave Evenson, head of the Wisconsin Sharp-Tailed Grouse

Society. The value of the Namekagon Barrens Wildlife Area is that it lies in the heart of this region.

The population has been too small, however, for the DNR to allow even a limited hunting season in recent years. DNR studies show numbers declined early in the twenty-first century and then stabilized at about two hundred dancing males, not enough, perhaps, to ensure a lasting population.

Year	Number of Dancing Male Grouse
2008	531
2010	289
2012	236
2014	191
2016	217
2018	117
2020	177
2022	178

Robert Hanson, Wisconsin DNR

Mike Amann, wildlife specialist for the Bayfield County Forestry and Parks Department, thinks the species has been undergoing a gradual decline of a few percent a year. Others, like Evenson, have argued that because grouse don't typically live a long time, a small, permitted hunting season would not be a detriment.

In 2011, the Wisconsin DNR noted that the genetic diversity of the grouse was not as great as in, for example, populations in Minnesota. Because they live in isolated "islands" on the landscape, the sharp-tailed grouse of Wisconsin are in danger of spiraling into an "extinction vortex" in which inbreeding results in less and less genetic diversity. That in turn can leave the species less able to adapt to change or stress.

County, state, and federal wildlife managers have gotten better in recent years at comparing notes and trying new steps to clear land, burn, and mow. They now talk about opening up new pockets of habitat, "stepping stones" a few miles apart that let birds move over greater distances and extend a grouse corridor throughout the Northwest Sands. From 2016 to 2018, the US Forest Service led an effort to bring more than 160 grouse from northwestern Minnesota into the Northwest Sands of Wisconsin. The birds were banded; some were fitted with radio transmitters to see how far they traveled.

Brian Heeringa, wildlife biologist for the US Forest Service and manager on the Moquah Barrens in Bayfield County, says that among the surprises was how quickly the birds dispersed. For example, some moved to

Sharp-tailed grouse are the flagship species on the barrens. Every spring, males do their best to impress females during their mating dance.

reuse an old dancing ground near an airport at Ashland. Another bird flew south to the Namekagon Barrens, some fifty miles. It was later shot by a hunter during open season but still stands as evidence of how quickly and how far sharp-tailed grouse can move to try to take advantage of available habitat. Whether the effort has driven the grouse population higher is too early to say, Heeringa thinks.

Not far away, Bayfield County foresters recently began applying the "stepping-stone" approach at Bass Lake near US Highway 2. Foresters are clearing and burning a 1,300-acre, mostly forested area that could become new barrens and one of the stepping stones. Not big enough to act as stand-alone grouse-breeding barrens, it nonetheless is close enough to the Barnes Barrens and the Moquah Barrens to give those grouse and other species a corridor to spread in. Likewise, state and Burnett County cooperation in clearing land next to the south unit of the Namekagon Barrens apparently has led to increased grouse in a section that hasn't seen a lot of grouse activity in recent years.

For now, the genetic diversity is sufficient for the birds to survive, Christel thinks, but it is questionable whether the population size is large enough to allow long-term survival on the barrens. Ultimately, if all goes well, she thinks the greatest population of sharp-tailed grouse will be found in the Moquah Barrens because there is more land there than at the Namekagon Barrens Wildlife Area.

So, after seventy years of active state management, the sharp-tailed grouse population on the barrens is short of healthy resurgence. At the same time, however, naturalists have adopted a shift in thinking. For one thing, the sense of rivalry among foresters, fire suppression specialists, and wildlife habitat specialists has diminished. Bruce Moss points out that foresters, too, are concerned about habitat and that fire suppression staffs now light the prescribed burns on the barrens. What in the 1950s might have been a clarion call to "save the sharp-tailed grouse" today is more often a "save the ecosystem" approach involving many kinds of plants and animals.

9

THE FERTILE BARRENS

The barrens, of course, are anything but barren. There's an abundance of life. The fun of exploring the barrens is discovering layer upon layer in an ecosystem brimming with species. Avid bird-watcher Jerry McAllister, a longtime visitor to the Namekagon Barrens, easily rattles off the names of dozens of birds you can see there—brown thrashers and towhees flitting through the brush, tree swallows and bluebirds vying for the two dozen birdhouses scattered across the wildlife area, warblers that fill the lowlands, ducks that swim in the wet spots, eagles and kestrels overhead, more than a half dozen sparrow species for diehard birders to identify. Most of these are not that hard to spot as you wander the barrens, depending on the time of year. But, as Jerry puts it, there are two "A-listers."

The sharp-tailed grouse, of course, is the reason the wildlife area is here. Aside from viewing the mating dance from the blinds in spring, you can often obtain good views as they sit quietly high in the few large pines that dot the landscape. They flush and fly noisily when you or your hunting dog get close in the brush. In fact, the barrens are a favorite place for hunting dog trials, events in which owners test their dogs' ability to perform in the field. In the past, a few hunters have been able to obtain DNR permits for grouse hunting, though not in recent years.

Harder to spot are the upland sandpipers. Sandpipers are normally shorebirds, but not these. Slender and tall, they stalk barrens and open land, hunting grasshoppers and other insects found there, particularly in areas that have been recently burned. These birds nest on the ground but often stand in trees and seem to enjoy making a circuit around you as they move from grass to tree and back.

(*Above*) Bluebirds and tree swallows vie for the several dozen wooden birdhouses put up in the wildlife area.

(*Right*) Bluebird eggs in the north unit.

Likewise, lots of mammals roam and scurry about the barrens, from deer to coyotes, fox, black bear, and the occasional moose. Even solitary mountain lions show up once in a great while. But to me there is one A-lister.

The gray wolf's story is often told. Once found throughout the northern forests, this species may have been eliminated in Wisconsin by the 1970s. As DNR wolf expert Jane Wiedenhoeft shared with me, the DNR found two wolves on the barrens in the winter of 1979–1980, but the species apparently disappeared again until 1996, when a pair wandered to the west side of the barrens from Minnesota. A pack of about seven wolves was centered on the barrens in 2007, and since then, other packs have moved around and used some of the barrens. Most recently, three packs of three to five members were using the wildlife area as part of their much larger territories. You seldom see a wolf on the barrens, but you can hear them howl at night, and you often find their four-inch tracks in the sand and the large, unmistakable piles of scat in the sandy roads. Once in a while, you

Brown thrashers love to flit among the brush.

come across a remaining leg
bone or two from a deer that
has been taken down. If it's
winter, the snow is marked all
around a kill site with wolf
urine.

Bird-watching is enticing
on the barrens, and seeing
wolves is always dramatic. But
you start to see the intricate
web of nature when you focus
on the plants. More than 180
species thrive in an environment whose harshness can
rival that of a desert.

Paul Hlina, a botanist who
has been studying and taking
plant inventories in the Northwest Sands for years, offers a
way to think about the plants,
clumping the main species on
the dry upland barrens into

Upland sandpipers are among the treats of ·
birdwatching on the barrens. LARRY DAU

several general groups. First is the scrub oak. You hear this term a lot.
Although elsewhere it can refer to a specific species, here on the Namekagon Barrens it is a reference to any short, stubby version of oak. There
are some sixty oak species in North America, and two dominate on the
barrens, where they take advantage of the acidic, sandy soil and sunny conditions. Hill's oak, also known as the northern pin oak (people typically
say "Hill's" when the tree is short and stubby), has pointy leaves with long,
broad gaps, or sinuses, between the lobes of the leaf. The second oak on
the barrens is the bur oak, a species of white oak that produces rounded
leaves that broaden toward the end. All oaks produce acorns, making them
a crucial link in the food chain on the barrens for birds and mammals.

Don't be fooled by how short the trees are. They have a wide root base
and grow quite old, regenerating growth again and again from the roots
after their tops have been killed by fire. A five-foot tree can be a hundred

(*Left*) Slanting sunlight shows wolf tracks on Springbrook Trail on a November day.

(*Below*) A trail camera on the north unit captures two barrens coyotes. COURTESY SNAPSHOT WISCONSIN/GARY DUNSMOOR

years old. The tough, thick root bases were the bane of farmers trying to grub them out (hence the sometimes-used name "grub" oak.)

Hlina groups two other plants with the scrub oaks for the roles they play in the network. Hazelnuts and prairie willow grow across the barrens, helping fill the role of low woody shrubs in providing food and cover for animals. Hazelnuts are especially aggressive spreaders. Larger, commercial hazelnuts are known as filberts. They are native to the barrens, but habitat specialists don't like to see these crowding out or shading

Scrub oaks, in this case a bur oak, are scattered across the wildlife area often standing only a few feet high because of frequent burning. They recover from the roots, sending new shoots up again and again.

Hill's oaks (*above*), also known as northern pin oaks, are identifiable by their pointed leaves, while the leaves of bur oaks (*right*) are more rounded.

the blueberries, grasses, and wildflowers. On the other hand, with a little labor you can eat these nuts. They grow in clusters of two or three and are at a height that makes them easy to reach without bending over. Unlike blueberries, they don't come ready to eat. You have to let them dry, and then you remove the husk. Cracking them can be difficult because they are hard and small. But they're one more way the barrens provide sustenance.

You probably think of willows as trees near water, bending long branches over streams or ponds. But the barrens are home to the prairie willow, which grows in thickets of three- to four-foot-high spears. They like sand and dry conditions and are often identifiable by the round insect galls that form on them.

Pines, of course, are legendary in these parts. Massive white pines along the rivers were logged heavily in the 1800s, but you don't find them much up on the barrens. You do find red pines, typically growing singly or in small stands, towering over the surrounding scrub oaks and brush. But the pine mainly identified with the barrens is the jack pine, smaller and with shorter needles than its more famous and beloved cousins. Like everything else here, it thrives in dry, sandy soil. And it is well adapted to fire. It doesn't grow back readily like oak after being top-killed, but some jack pines have cones that spring open in a fire and seed new trees. These are known as serotinous cones. (There is actually a geographic distribution of these jack pine types: serotinous jack pines tend to grow north of Wisconsin Highway 70, according to the DNR's Ben Garrett.) Throw a hard, tight jack pine cone into a campfire and watch it quickly open up and release the seeds inside. It's been estimated that an acre of jack pine forest is carrying two million seeds waiting for a fire. Along with the oaks, these are the plants that remind you: this is not a grassland or a prairie, it is a forest in its early stages. Jack pine cones can release their seeds when the sand heats on a hot summer day, but left alone and without fire, these pines would eventually be shaded out and replaced by red pines. With repeated fire, they flourish.

In late summer, jack pines become a gathering place for monarch butterflies preparing for their long migration to Mexico. The butterflies like pines to roost in as they gather strength.

Blueberries, sweet fern, sand cherries, and New Jersey tea are the main low-growing bushes found in patches all around the barrens. There are

Fires can kill the mature jack pines, but their cones open after a fire and reseed themselves.

lots of reasons to visit the barrens; picking blueberries is one of the best. Lowbush blueberry bushes, standing one to one and a half feet high, thrive in sandy, low-nutrient soil. They love terrain kept sunny by frequent burning. They outcompete plants nearby because they take advantage of fungi called mycorrhizae that essentially extend their root systems. These fungi pass along nutrients and water in exchange for sugars made by the plant. (This complex arrangement is one reason transplanting them to your yard is difficult.) For generations, people have been coming in July, searching for the best patches and picking the small ripe fruits. Some years' crops are better than others, and patience is rewarded as you search. But when you do find a good patch, bushes are so loaded that you can grab handfuls at a time for your pancakes, muffins, jam, and more. For the Ojibwe,

(*Above*) Sand cherries show off their pink-white blossoms in spring.

(*Left*) Blueberries ripen in July.

blueberries have been a reason to return to the barrens seasonally for generations. For immigrants and other homesteaders a hundred years ago, the berries were often their best cash crop. One old-timer recalled picking in the 1930s, saying a family could pick twenty to thirty quarts in a day and make three dollars.

To some people, the smell of the barrens is sweet fern, especially on a warm summer day. A fragrant member of the bayberry family, sweet ferns' serrated dark green leaves might remind you of the hemp plant, but they aren't related. It's not a fern either. Instead, it acts like a legume, meaning it enriches the soil, pulling nitrogen out of the air via bacteria on its roots. Sweet ferns are like blueberries in that they grow close to the ground, love nutrient-poor sandy soil, and thrive after an area has been burned or otherwise disturbed.

Sand cherries fill the barrens with white blossoms in May and June, just as the land is greening up from spring rains. Typically, you find them early in the barrens-forest succession. Once trees start, the sand cherries fade until the next burn. The fruit is purple to black when it ripens, much like a chokecherry or a pin cherry. As with those cherries,

Junegrass blooms in June on the south unit. PHOTO BY LISA PETERS

Cotton grass is actually a sedge, and its fluffy white seed heads adorn large sedge meadows in wet areas in June.

the sand cherries are edible but they are strong-tasting and have a pit you want to get rid of before you make jelly.

New Jersey tea is another one- to three-foot-tall plant common on the barrens. It has served medicinal purposes for Ojibwe people, blooming with white flowers from June through August. It is sometimes known as redroot.

Again, the barrens are not grasslands, but you can find a variety of native grasses there. In the cool season there is Kalm's brome with its sheaths, or stems, drooping and nodding to the side, and Junegrass, which appropriately becomes visible in June, showing off long clusters of flowers. Then through the summer you see big bluestem and little bluestem, switchgrass, and, in slight depressions, Indian grass.

A lot of what you first think are grasses on the barrens are really sedges. They tend to have triangular blades. ("Sedges have edges," the saying goes.) They grow small but interesting tufts that are the plant's flowers. Some, like the common Pennsylvania sedge or the Richardson's sedge, like the

A single wood lily shows its color beneath a lone jack pine.

Hoary puccoon (*left*) blossoms in spring, blue asters (*above*) in fall.

dry, sandy uplands. Others prefer low, wet spots. In spring, for example, when you look down into the bog on the south unit, you see thousands of round, white balls spread across the terrain. These are cotton grass, actually a sedge.

Dozens of flowering plants (or forbs, in botany lingo) grace the barrens through the year and distinguish these barrens from the sandy pine barrens of, say, New Jersey. There are pale purple pasqueflowers poking out of the sand after snowmelt, delicate prairie buttercups, bright yellow hairy and hoary puccoon, purple phlox and birdsfoot violets in spring; orange butterfly flower and hairy-looking, bee-attracting blue bergamot in summer; sunflowers and asters in September; and many more. The showiest of the crop are the wood lilies. Two-and-a-half inches across and with six deep fiery orange petals, the blossoms rise one to three feet out of the surrounding grass and sedge, not typically in big groups but instead appearing here and there to surprise you as you walk the barrens.

The barrens are natural pollinator gardens, Hlina says, and the fifty to sixty flowering plants that are native are of course key to the food chain, attracting the insects that let birds and small mammals survive. Two flowers you'll be lucky to see are arbutus and lupine. When Europeans arrived in this area, they found a fragrant, low white flower known as the trailing arbutus. They picked it enthusiastically, enjoying its scent, drying it, and even selling it commercially. Unfortunately, the flower was overpicked and you find its unobtrusive bloom in the spring only rarely today. It likes the woods nearby more than the barrens themselves.

Not far south of the Namekagon Barrens you can find wild lupines in profusion, growing their purple spikes of multiple flowers in the woods, in roadside ditches, and in cabin yards. But not in the barrens. A patch grows on the far southern boundary of the south unit, tucked onto a south-facing hillside not far from Dogtown Creek. But that's about it in the barrens. Why this sharp "northern lupine line"? It's not clear, but perhaps there is a temperature gradient that won't allow the native lupine to extend its range farther north. If that is the case, it will be interesting to see whether climate change extends the range. Lupines are the sole food for caterpillars of the endangered Karner blue butterfly. My wife, Lisa, and I have seen these lovely small butterflies just a few miles south of the barrens but they have never been recorded in the wildlife area.

Lupines grow in only one place on the barrens, at the south side of the south unit.

And that's just the dry upland brushy area that dominates the wildlife area, a demanding environment for plants.

On the south unit of the wildlife area is an equally demanding and harsh environment: wet, acidic bogs and open water in one low spot. Here spruce trees and tamarack keep their roots in water virtually year round. Sphagnum moss covers big areas, growing in inches-deep water. Plants like bog rosemary, bog laurel, wild cranberries, and insectivorous pitcher plants and sundew thrive. It's another world for those willing to get their feet wet.

Wild cranberries (*left*) and pitcher plants (*right*) grace the south unit bog. Here, the odd-shaped leaves of a pitcher plant emerge from a mat of sphagnum moss.

If you're lucky enough to take a walk with Hlina, you don't get very far very fast. Have him throw down his meter-square quadrant and you won't move for an hour or two.

Inside that white plastic square will be a universe that first looks chaotic but then slowly resolves into a field lab. In one spot, you'll see stems of foot-tall blazing stars starting to open, the low green leaves of asters not yet blooming, sedges and big bluestem grass, wild roses and a kind of artemisia known as wormwood. Frostweed isn't showing its big yellow blossom but instead exhibits a reproduction strategy for tougher times: a smaller, less showy, closed flower. A dozen species are there, twice the number you'd find in the nearby woods, according to Hlina.

Then pick up the quadrant, walk across the road, and throw it down

Botanist Paul Hlina, top center, directs a handful of enthusiasts in the fine art of barrens plant identification.

again into a whole new universe, perhaps one burned more recently than your first try. Here is a small grub oak, bearberries, wood betony, sand cherries, miniscule white flowers known as bluets. You can debate which sunflower you have, western or woodland.

Do this and you see the mosaic nature of the barrens on display. One thing here, another thing there. And next year it will be something else again.

10

Let's Take a Walk

For a number of years, the Friends of the Namekagon Barrens Wildlife Area has supported the mission of the DNR. The group handles grouse blind reservations, organizes gatherings and nature walks, built a picnic shelter, put up signs and information boards, and created an auto tour to help people get acquainted.

But nothing beats just getting out on the barrens for a walk. The wildlife area contains no maintained trails so hiking here is more a choose-your-own-adventure experience. Head out where you want to; see what you can see. Remember that the views change depending on how recently an area has been burned.

Also remember: you're on foot. ATVs are not the best way to see the barrens. At this writing, they are allowed on township roads but not on the wildlife area's fire lanes nor across the barrens themselves, where riders have been doing increasing amounts of damage. A last admonition: don't dig up the wildflowers to plant in your yard. Even seed collecting is frowned upon for fear that too many seeds will be taken from the barrens.

Here's a suggested route that takes you a mile and a half across the heart of the north unit, with a sampling of geology, history, botany, and land management starting near Evergreen Cemetery on Five Mile Road. In January, put on your snowshoes; in the fall, think twice or at least wear blaze orange so the hunters see you.

An October view of the south unit bog from Namekagon Trail.

EVERGREEN CEMETERY

The last person was buried here more than a hundred years ago. In fact, the three-acre cemetery was mostly out of sight until the DNR mistakenly started to prepare it for clearing several decades ago. Most of those who

A flag flies over Evergreen Cemetery on Five Mile Road.

were interred lie now in unmarked graves. Big boulders—incongruous in this land of sand—protect the graveyard from ATV riders. A flag flies and a stone marker pays homage to the lives of American Indians and white farmers who once inhabited the barrens. It's estimated that more than two dozen people lie here. Walk south toward the back of the three-acre plot to find the only marked graves. One concrete marker, barely legible, names Anna B. Cole, about whom virtually nothing is known, other than the eroding dates, 1856–1906. Another is a rock with white painted letters rubbing away. Once they said *Anderson babies*, marking the location of five children buried by one family. The only other marker is a metal sign hanging from a wire, the words *Arvid Lyons* stamped on it. His 1903 farm lay just over a small hill a mile from here.

HUMPHREY HILLOCK'S DEPRESSION

Cross Five Mile Road from the cemetery and you hike down ten feet or so into a depression. Imagine the block of ice that once sat here, covered with glacial outwash sand that collapsed as the ice melted, leaving a kettle that stays a little more moist than the surrounding hillsides. More recent history: this is one tiny parcel of the hundreds of thousands of acres awarded to a predecessor of the Chicago, St. Paul, Minneapolis & Omaha Railway as an incentive to build a railroad from St. Croix Falls to Superior and Bayfield.

Take your time; make a small circuit on the hillside around the depression. The dominant plants are bur oaks just a few feet tall; notice that in some places they are thick and clustered while in others there are grassy openings among them. Jack pines are here but they are short seedlings. Sand cherries with their red stems

Kalm's brome seeds in July on the north unit.

stand eight to twelve inches tall, especially prevalent up the slope where the shade of oaks preserves moisture. Big bluestem, Kalm's brome, and Pennsylvania sedge are here. The low plants with glossy leaves are bearberries. Brushy New Jersey tea blooms white in spring; hazelnuts push in around some of the oaks. Goldenrod and western sunflowers add yellow splashes in summer and fall. Silvery white sage sends up spears that stand out from the green.

DRY LANDING ROAD

Walk up out of the slight depression, traveling west a few feet to Dry Landing Road, and continue north about a tenth of a mile. This is a good place to compare the Burnett County forest land on the west side of the road with the state-owned wildlife area to the east. It's the same terrain—glacial outwash sands spread across a plain.

(*Above*) White-tailed deer, this one captured on a trail cam, make frequent use of the wildlife area. COURTESY SNAPSHOT WISCONSIN/GARY DUNSMOOR

(*Left*) Tree swallows perform a mating ritual in the north unit.

Look west, and your gaze can't penetrate more than a few feet into the forest. It's hard to believe, but this was once the homestead of Joseph and Sarah Gage (parents of Ruby Hillock, married to Benjamin Hillock and living just up the road for a while). Now it is growing trees for future sale by the county. It was planted in red pine in 1941, and planted again in 1989, mostly in red pine but some jack pine and hardwoods. It's due for thinning sometime around the mid-2020s, likely as pulpwood.

Now turn and face east from the road, and you can look out for a mile or more at a mix of stubby bur oak and Hill's oak, land that is burned regularly. Deer roam (including one that collided with my car right here as I was arriving one night in 2021 to appreciate the dark sky), grouse nest, and kestrels, bluebirds, and tree swallows soar. About two-tenths of a mile up the road from the cemetery, stop and either squint hard or use your imagination: this is where the stagecoach road lay in the 1850s and 1860s, crossing your path from southwest to northeast.

Benjamin and Ruby Hillock's Farm

You can either hike kitty corner to the northeast about four-tenths of a mile (this is the stagecoach road route) or take Dry Landing Road north and turn east on St. Croix Trail. Either way, you come to the one-time farm of Benjamin and Ruby Hillock on the north side of the road. About all that's left is the six- to eight-foot-deep depression of what was either the house or a barn, about thirty feet by twenty, its corners marked by rocks. This is a good place to look across the barrens to the south and east and north. The terrain is mostly flat and uncollapsed, good evidence of the massive flows of glacial outwash streams that laid down hundreds of feet of sand fourteen thousand years ago.

Forest Home School

The Hillock children undoubtedly attended school right next door, where the schoolhouse foundation still lies on the north side of St. Croix Trail. It has a front step, a vestibule, and a wall down the middle. So perhaps it was a two-room schoolhouse. The children of the community of Five Mile attended here, arriving by horse, by foot, by sleigh. Every year or two from 1906 to 1938, a new young woman arrived to teach. The school burned down in 1931, was rebuilt, and finally closed the same year the last settler was moved out by the federal government. If you get here at the right time in April and May, you can find lovely pale purple pasqueflowers, one of the first signs that winter has let go of the barrens for another year. Later in the spring and summer, watch for bluebirds using the box at the back of the foundation.

CLEMENS CREEK RAVINE

Get yourself behind the schoolhouse foundation, the north side, and start walking northeast. Again, you are pretty much on the old stagecoach road and you can definitely see the ruts made 150 years ago, at least in places. Depending on the time of year this is an easy walk or a bit of a slog through hazelnut and scrub oak. It also depends on how recently the land was burned. Eventually, after several hundred yards, you start down a slight incline in which the stagecoach ruts are quite evident, almost a foot deep and eight feet apart. The route leads you to a small stand of mature jack pine.

But here's a puzzle: to your left is the beginning of a marshy ravine, essentially the headwaters of Clemens Creek. It can be deceptively wet. You start across it, even in winter, and find yourself over your boots in water that eventually makes its way to the St. Croix River a few miles west. To your right is a grassy pond, also full of water and impassable. But here in front of you is a ten-foot-wide berm that lets you push through the aspen and prairie willow, keep your feet dry, and get across the ravine. Why? Did the stagecoach road builders create it? Did the homesteaders make a dam to hold back water they could use? Or has it always been this way? This is the place to use your imagination.

GOMULAK FIRE LANE

Once you get across the berm and past the pond, keep bearing to the northeast. You're still on the stagecoach road, and you get glimpses of

Signs mark the intersection of two fire lanes used to help contain
prescribed fires. MARK NUPEN

still-packed soil with sparse vegetation and occasional ruts. In a few hundred yards you hit the DeLong-Lien Fire Lane (named for two men who devoted years to caring for and preserving the wildlife area). Keep going another couple hundred yards to Gomulak Fire Lane. Again you can see the kettles that formed when blocks of glacial ice melted and the sand on top collapsed. You might spot ducks in the wet spots; you might see wolf tracks on Gomulak. This can be a good place to be in July when the blueberries are ripe.

If you retrace your steps from here, you've covered a little more than three miles round trip back to the cemetery. Or you can keep going to the northeast, following the occasional visible stagecoach ruts and skirting more wet kettles until you reach County Line Road north of No Man's Lake, the line between Burnett and Washburn Counties. This makes your walk about three miles one way.

That's just one way to walk the barrens. If you want more of a challenge, hike down into the bog on the south unit for a springtime look at pitcher

The south unit features a bog some one hundred feet below Springbrook Trail and Namekagon Trail, ringed by tamarack and spruce. MARK NUPEN

plants, sphagnum moss, tamarack, and spruce. Bring your rain boots or old tennis shoes. Or walk the north side of the south unit, taking off from the wildlife area to the big bend in the Namekagon River for a look at where the old bridge crossed. Then again, you could walk the south side of the south unit, looking for those northernmost lupines, or follow the north side of Rand Creek in the north unit looking for spring warblers. Or find an asparagus plant that maybe Bertena Krause planted just off Gomulak Fire Lane . . . or just stop anywhere and wander to see what sand and fire have done.

Epilogue

I haven't seen the woman from Spooner again, the one who stood up amid the blueberries and wondered where she was. I hope she and her kids enjoyed their pie. I went back to that patch a year later. Where I had pulled berries off bushes by the handful there was not a one.

A late frost and a prolonged dry spell apparently had done in the berries for that year. Nothing quite stays the same on this landscape.

You can pick just about any place on Earth and do what I have done with the Forest Home School on the Namekagon Barrens. Look back in time, get down on your hands and knees, take photos, see where on the horizon the full moon rises in June, search the internet, talk to people about it, read and contemplate how nature and history weave together on the land.

Here in the barrens, starting with that initial moment of awakening—wait, this isn't supposed to look like this, is it?—the story that emerges is that the Namekagon Barrens are worth preserving. Why not even enlarge them, at least by continuing to add open "stepping stones" throughout the Northwest Sands?

This area does not look exactly like it did two hundred years ago. There are roads and square corners; the burning is regimented and more frequent than it was before Europeans arrived in large numbers. But still, this is among the few places you can look around today and say, more or less, that this has the look and feel that it did when Indigenous people were the only ones on the land.

It's not wilderness, but it's wild, an assemblage of plants, animals, and human history that intertwine uniquely, driven largely by two forces: sand and fire.

Geology gave us the sand, which in turn dictated what people have done here. And what they have done forms a microcosm of American history—Indigenous seasonal rounds, westward expansion and dispossession, immigration, Dust Bowl hardscrabble farming, continued hunting and gathering, and the emergence of an environmental ethic.

A red pine stands as a sentinel over the open barrens terrain on the south unit of the Namekagon Barrens Wildlife Area.

But it has taken active management to put the natural process of fire back. Prescribed burning has made the barrens today a showcase for understanding how nature weaves together its strands of life and then for taking action to maintain the web that results. It seems odd to say it, but once we decide we need to fight wildfires, without active intervention this ecosystem is lost.

Of course, climate change will likely dictate the terms of the future. Since the middle of the twentieth century, changes in temperature and precipitation have been more pronounced in the barrens and northwestern Wisconsin than in the rest of the state. The average annual temperature at the barrens rose two degrees between 1950 and 2006. Winter temperatures rose even faster, and the growing season is nearly a month longer. While other parts of Wisconsin grew wetter over that time period, the barrens have seen declining precipitation.

What do these changes mean for the jack pines and scrub oaks that dominate the barrens today? Will erratic spring melting and freezing disrupt grouse roosting? Will wilder weather elsewhere disrupt migration patterns for birds that use the barrens? Will the ranges of flowers and other plants expand or contract, creating different kinds of competition? Could lupines, for example, move farther north into the barrens and bring rare Karner blue butterflies with them? Will berry crops be diminished by earlier springs combined with late frosts? Will invasive plants move in more readily? Can we use the barrens to learn about resilience?

Maintaining a vibrant barrens will give us the opportunity to answer these questions and more.

ACKNOWLEDGMENTS

For such a short book, I owe much to many.

First are my friends from the Friends. The Friends of the Namekagon Barrens Wildlife Area supports the mission of the Wisconsin DNR at the barrens. To me, however, the group is most valuable as a forum for comparing notes and telling one another the last thing you saw or found out about the barrens. So, to Vern Drake (the baron of the barrens), Mark Nupen (who dragged me into the group and has unflagging enthusiasm for the barrens), Gary Dunsmoor (who I believe has spent more hours on the barrens than anyone else alive), Kathy Bartilson (organizer in chief), and Jerry McAllister (master of birds and bird dogs), thanks for sharing and thanks for including some results of my research on the Friends website.

Nancy Christel, who has managed the wildlife area for the DNR for years, was extremely generous with her time and expertise and records, starting the day I walked into the office in Spooner asking lots of questions and exhibiting my ignorance. Nancy and many others, active and retired, at the DNR, the US Forest Service, and county offices showed again and again that they truly know their stuff, from wolves to fire to ecosystems. You're impressive.

Highlights of my research have been the ability to spend time on the barrens with Brian Finstad, local historian extraordinaire and the best there is at spotting subtle tracks left by stagecoaches 150 years ago, and Paul Hlina, research botanist, native plant expert, and patient teacher of the difference between hairy puccoon and hoary puccoon.

Many others also gave their time to help me. Thanks to Mike Amann, Jim Anderson, Jerry Bartelt, Bob Birmingham, Owen Boyle, Tom Fitz, Bob Hanson, Ben Garrett, Brian Heeringa, Virgil Hillock Sr., Jason Holmes, John Jenson, Sherry Kell, John Lambert, Thomas Loebel, Mike Luedeke, Donald Monson, Bruce Moss, Jake Nichols, Beatrice Roatch, Carol Smith, Anton Treuer, Dave Ullman, and Dawn White. Thanks also to Martin Remus and his pals at the Minnesota Genealogical Society for help finding and translating Swedish records. And of course there's nothing like a good librarian. Thanks to the librarians and archivists at the Wisconsin

Historical Society Library in Madison, the Chalmer Davee Library at the University of Wisconsin at River Falls, and the Burnett County Historical Society in Danbury.

I'm especially grateful to the people who took the time to read part or all of my manuscript-in-the-making—Tom Weber, Lisa Peters, Gary Dunsmoor, Tom Fitz, John Lambert, Ryan O'Connor, Brian Finstad, Mike Luedeke and, in particular, Edith Leoso, the tribal history preservation officer at the Bad River Band of Lake Superior Chippewa. Thank you, Edith, for trying to teach me the idea of *debwe*, to speak the truth.

All of you have my great appreciation. Needless to say, all shortcomings of this work are my own.

I spent much of my career in journalism trying to convince people that everyone needs an editor. It's been my great fortune that this project has landed in very capable hands at the Wisconsin Historical Society Press, starting with those of director Kate Thompson, who championed the effort. Editors Sara Phillips and Rachel Cordasco and copy editor Melissa York have done nothing but improve it.

This wouldn't have been anything more than idle chit chat without my wife, Lisa. A gifted writer, a wonderful editor, and a boon barrens companion, Lisa encouraged and encouraged and encouraged. You have my love and appreciation. I finally get to turn the tables and dedicate a book to you.

Bibliography

Articles and Presentations

Birmingham, Robert. "Dogtown: A Historical and Archaeological Study of a Late Historic St. Croix Chippewa Community," *Wisconsin Archaeologist* 65, no. 3 (1984): 201.

Christel, Nancy. "Namekagon Barrens Wildlife Area Lease History." Wisconsin DNR memo. February 24, 2009. Provided by Nancy Christel, Wisconsin DNR office, Spooner.

Clayton, Lee. "Pleistocene Geology of the Superior Region, Wisconsin." 1984. University of Wisconsin–Extension. Information Circular No. 46. Wisconsin Geological and Natural History Survey.

"County May Lose North and South Trunk Highway; Proposed Routes Straight East from Grantsburg." *Burnett County Enterprise* (Webster, Wisconsin), September 20, 1917.

"Crex Meadows Wildlife Area." Wisconsin DNR website. https://dnr.wisconsin .gov/topic/Lands/WildlifeAreas/crex.html.

"Death Takes Miss Hillock in Seattle." *Webster City (IA) Freeman*, October 4, 1941.

"Douglas County Wildlife Area." Douglas County, Wisconsin website. www .douglascountywi.org/245/Douglas-County-Wildlife-Area.

Finstad, Brian. Oral presentations to the Friends of the Namekagon Barrens Wildlife Area, July 20, 2019, and July 17, 2021.

Fitz, Tom. Geology professor, Northland College. Guided field trip for Minnesota Geological Society, September 8 and 9, 2019.

Goldfield, Anna. "Five Breakthrough Signs of Early Peoples in North America." *Sapiens*, November 4, 2021. www.sapiens.org/column/field-trips/earliest -people-north-america/.

Gregg, Larry, and Neal D. Niemuth. "The History, Status, and Future of Sharp-Tailed Grouse in Wisconsin." *Passenger Pigeon* 62, no. 2 (2000): 158–174.

Guyette, Richard P., Michael C. Stambaugh, Daniel C. Dey, Joseph M. Marschall, Jay Saunders, and John Lampereur. "350 Years of Fire-Climate-Human

Interactions in a Great Lakes Sandy Outwash Plain." *Forests* 7, no. 9 (2016). https://doi.org/10.3390/f7090189.

Hanson, Bob. Wisconsin DNR wildlife biologist. Public presentation. Douglas County Wildlife Area, May 24, 2022.

Hillock, Humphrey. Obituary. *Webster City Freeman* (Iowa), July 23, 1911.

Jordahl, Harold C., Jr. "Public Land Use Planning and Policy Formulation in Wisconsin: A Case Study of Prairie Grouse Management Problems." 1955. Draft of report. Provided by Nancy Christel, Wisconsin DNR office, Spooner.

Kane, Lucile M. "Settling the Wisconsin Cutovers," *Wisconsin Magazine of History* 40, no. 2 (1956–57): 91–98.

Lambert, John M. "Upper Valley Dalton at the Sucices Site in Northwest Wisconsin." *Wisconsin Archaeologist* 95, no. 2 (2014): 152–157.

Lambert, John M. and Thomas J. Loebel. "Cody Complex Foragers on the Eastern Fringe: Scottsbluff and Hardin in the Western Great Lakes." Paper presented at the 87th Annual Society for American Archeology Conference, Chicago, Illinois, April 1, 2022.

Meunier, Jed, Nathon S. Holoubek, and Megan Sebasky. "Fire Regime Characteristics in Relation to Physiography at Local and Landscape Scales in Lake States Pine Forests." *Forest Ecology and Management* 454, December 2019. https://doi.org/10.1016/j.foreco.2019.117651.

Monmonier, Mark. "Aerial Photography at the Agricultural Adjustment Administration: Acreage Controls, Conservation Benefits, and Overhead Surveillance in the 1930s." *Photogrammetric Engineering & Remote Sensing*, December 2002, 1257–1261.

Murphy, Raymond E. "Geography of the Northwestern Pine Barrens of Wisconsin." *Transactions of the Wisconsin Academy of Sciences, Arts and Letters* 26 (1931): 69–122.

Nowell, R. I. "Experience of Resettlement Administration Program in Lakes States." *Journal of Farm Economics* 19, no. 1 (February 1937): 206–233.

"Overland from St. Paul to Lake Superior," *Harper's New Monthly Magazine*, December 1863.

Satz, Ronald N. "The 1837 Pine Tree Treaty." *Chippewa Treaty Rights: The Reserved Rights of Wisconsin's Chippewa Indians in Historical Perspective.* Madison: Wisconsin Academy of Arts, Sciences and Letters, 1991. 13–31.

Sorden, L. G. "The Northern Wisconsin Settler Relocation Project, 1934–1940." *Proceedings of the Fourth Annual Meeting of the Forest History Association of Wisconsin, Inc., September 28–29, 1979.* Wausau, Wisconsin. Edited by Ramon R. Hernandez.

"They Just Kept Shooting: Zach Survived Malmedy Massacre." *Spooner* (WI) *Advocate*, Nov. 7, 2002.

"Who We Are: A History of the St. Croix People." St. Croix Chippewa Indians of Wisconsin website. https://stcroixojibwe-nsn.gov/culture/who-we-are/.

BOOKS

Benton-Banai, Edward. *The Mishomis Book: The Voice of the Ojibway*. Minneapolis: University of Minnesota Press, 2010.

Chamberlin, T. C. *Geology of Wisconsin: Survey of 1873–1879*. Madison: State of Wisconsin Commissioners of Public Printing, 1883.

Child, Brenda. *Holding Our World Together: Ojibwe Women and the Survival of Community*. Penguin Library of American Indian History. New York: Penguin, 2012.

Child, Brenda. *My Grandfather's Knocking Sticks: Ojibwe Family Life and Labor on the Reservation*. St. Paul: Minnesota Historical Society Press, 2014.

Connor, Lafayette. *Cecilia: The Trials of an Amazing Ojibwe Woman, 1834–1892*. Danbury, WI: Burnett County Historical Society, 2006.

Corneli, Helen McGavran. *Mice in the Freezer, Owls on the Porch: The Lives of Naturalists Frederick and Frances Hamerstrom*. Madison: University of Wisconsin Press, 2006.

Curtis, John T. *Vegetation of Wisconsin: An Ordination of Plant Communities*. Madison: University of Wisconsin Press, 1959.

Densmore, Frances. *Strength of the Earth*. St. Paul: Minnesota Historical Society Press, 2005.

Gilchrist, Susan Cantrell. *Sand Country Memories: Oral Perspectives of Wisconsin's Northwest Pine Barrens*. Madison: Bureau of Science Services, Wisconsin Department of Natural Resources, 2008.

Gough, Robert. *Farming the Cutover, A Social History of Northern Wisconsin, 1900–1940*. Lawrence, Kansas: University Press of Kansas, 1997.

Grange, Wallace B. *Wisconsin Grouse Problems*. Madison: Wisconsin Conservation Department, 1948.

Grover, Linda LeGarde. *Onigamiising: Seasons of an Ojibwe Year*. Minneapolis: University of Minnesota Press, 2017.

Hamerstrom, Frederick, Frances Hamerstrom, and Oswald Mattson. *Sharptails into the Shadows?* Madison: Game Management Division, Wisconsin Department Conservation, 1952.

Helgeson, Arlen. *Farms in the Cutover: Agricultural Settlement in Northern Wisconsin*. Madison: State Historical Society of Wisconsin, 1962.

LaBerge, Gene L. *Geology of the Lake Superior Region*. Phoenix, AZ: Geoscience Press, Inc., 1994.

Larson, Lars Erik. *The Enduring Cutover: Contributions to the History of Wisconsin's Northern Region*. Whitewater, WI: self-published, 2016. www .chequamegonbay-history.com/files/EnduringCutover_LELarson.pdf.

Loew, Patty. *Indian Nations of Wisconsin: Histories of Endurance and Renewal*. 2nd Rev. Ed. Madison: Wisconsin Historical Society Press, 2013.

Monson, Donald L. *The Namekagon Bridge 1863–1941*. Spooner, Wisconsin: self-published, 2020.

Norrgard, Chantal. *Seasons of Change: Labor, Treaty Rights and Ojibwe Nationhood*. Chapel Hill: University of North Carolina Press, 2014.

Raff, Jennifer. *Origin: A Genetic History of the Americas*. New York: Hachette Book Group, 2022.

Seningen, Ron. *Mr. Gordon's Neighborhood: An Illustrated Timeline of the Gordon and Wascott Communities and Adjacent Northwestern Wisconsin Before, During, and After the Days of Antoine Gordon*. Eau Claire, WI: self-published, 2010.

Treuer, Anton. *Ojibwe in Minnesota*. St. Paul: Minnesota Historical Society Press, 2010.

Treuer, David. *The Heartbeat of Wounded Knee: Native America from 1890 to the Present*. New York: Riverhead Books, 2019.

Warren, William. *History of the Ojibway People*. 1885. Reprint, St. Paul: Minnesota Historical Society Press, 2009.

Westerman, Gwen, and Bruce White. *Mni Sota Makoce: The Land of the Dakota*. St. Paul: Minnesota Historical Society Press, 2012.

Wingerd, Mary Lethert. *North Country: The Making of Minnesota*. Minneapolis: University of Minnesota Press, 2010.

Wisconsin Department of Natural Resources. *Ecological Landscape of Wisconsin: An Assessment of Ecological Resources and a Guide to Planning*

Sustainable Management. PUB-SS-1131H 2017. Madison, Wisconsin, 2017. Chapter 2, Assessment of Current Condition; Chapter 7, Natural Communities, Aquatic Features; and Chapter 17, Northwest Sands Ecological Landscape. https://dnr.wisconsin.gov/topic/Lands/Book.html.

Zwinger, Ann H. *Run, River, Run: A Naturalist's Journey Down One of the Great Rivers of the West*. Tucson: University of Arizona Press, 1984.

GOVERNMENT AND GENEALOGY RECORDS

Annual Enumeration of Farm Statistics for Blaine Township for US Department of Agriculture and the State of Wisconsin, 1923, 1924, 1925, 1926, 1927, 1928, 1929, 1930, 1931, 1936, 1939. Microfilm. Chalmer Davee Library, University of Wisconsin–River Falls.

Birth, marriage, and emigration records from churches in Norrbarke, Kumla, and Soderbarke, Sweden, including the *Kumla Household Examination Record*. Digitized archives accessed via Swedish records expert Martin Remus at the Minnesota Genealogical Society in Mendota Heights, Minnesota.

Blaine Township burial and death records. Burnett County Historical Society, Forts Folle Avoine, Danbury, Wisconsin.

Blaine Township election records, 1906–1972. Burnett County Historical Society, Forts Folle Avoine, Danbury, Wisconsin.

Burnett County death records. Burnett County Historical Society, Forts Folle Avoine, Danbury, Wisconsin.

Burnett County land records. Register of Deeds, Burnett County, Wisconsin. County office building, Siren, Wisconsin.

Evergreen Cemetery burial records. Compiled by Vern Drake. Blaine Township. Burnett County Historical Society, Danbury, Wisconsin.

Find-A-Grave memorial. Ancestry.com

Land patents. Bureau of Land Management, Records of the General Land Office. 1890–1950. https://glorecords.blm.gov/.

Land sale records. Chicago, St. Paul, Minneapolis & Omaha Railway Archives, Berwyn, Illinois.

Manifest of *SS Cymric* from Liverpool, England, to New York, Arriving August 24, 1903. Minnesota Genealogical Society. Mendota Heights, Minnesota.

Minnesota Marriages Index, 1849–1950. Ancestry.com

Peet, Ed. "Burnett County, Wisconsin: A Pamphlet Descriptive of Northern Wisconsin in General and of Burnett County in Detail." Burnett County

Board of Immigration 1902 Report. Wisconsin Historical Society Archives, Madison, Wisconsin.

Standard Atlas of Burnett County, Wisconsin. Commonly known as the county plat book. Chicago: Geo. A. Ogle & Co., 1915. Republished, Shell Lake, Wisconsin: Burnett County Historical Society and White Birch Printing Inc., 1985.

US Census Records, Arkansas. California Township, Cleburne County, 1920. Ancestry.com.

US Census Records, Iowa. Webster City, 1870, 1900, and 1910. Geneva, 1880 and 1900. Ancestry.com.

US Census Records, Minnesota. Chisholm, 1930. Tara Township, Traverse County, 1920. White Pine Township, Aitkin County, 1930. Ancestry.com.

US Census Records, New Mexico. St. Vrain, Curry County, 1930. Ancestry. com.

US Census Records, North Dakota. Rugby, 1920 and 1940. Roberts County, 1940. Ancestry.com.

US Census Records, Wisconsin. Blaine Township, 1880, 1890, 1900, 1910, 1920, 1930, and 1940. Cedarburg, 1930. Cumberland, 1930. Meenon, 1920. Milwaukee, 1900 and 1920. Minong Township, 1910. Minong, 1910. Rusk, 1900. Siren, 1940. Walworth, 1880. Ancestry.com.

US Census Records, Wyoming. Sheridan, 1920. Ancestry.com.

US World War I draft registration cards. Ancestry.com.

Wisconsin birth and death records. Ancestry.com.

Wisconsin Marriage Index, 1808–1907. Ancestry.com.

Wisconsin Marriage Index, 1904. Ancestry.com.

Wisconsin Post Office Handbook: 1821–1971. Compiled by James B. Hale. Bulletin No. 10-1971. Wisconsin Postal History Society, Green Bay, Wisconsin.

Wisconsin Post Office Handbook: 1821–1971. Compiled by James B. Hale. Bulletin No. 10-1971. Wisconsin Postal History Society, Green Bay, Wisconsin.

Wisconsin State Census Records. Blaine Township, 1905. Ancestry.com.

Wisconsin State Census Records. Blaine Township, 1905. Rusk Township, 1905. Ancestry.com.

Wyoming death records. Ancestry.com.

INTERVIEWS

Amann, Mike. Bayfield County Forestry and Parks administrator. Phone interview, April 6, 2021.

Anderson, Jim. Son of Fred and Mildred Zach Anderson. Interview, June 5, 2018, Sand Lake, Washburn County, Wisconsin.

Bartelt, Jerry. Retired wildlife biologist, Wisconsin DNR. Phone interview, July 2, 2021.

Birmingham, Robert. Former Wisconsin state archaeologist. Phone interview, January 16, 2019.

Boyle, Owen. Species management section chief, Wisconsin DNR. Phone interview, June 25, 2021.

Breckenridge, Andy. Geology professor, University of Wisconsin–Superior. Phone interview, April 13, 2019.

Christel, Nancy. Wildlife manager, Wisconsin DNR. Interview, January 17, 2020, Spooner, Wisconsin. Phone interviews, May 28, 2020, and April 28, 2021.

Drake, Vern. Resident just east of the barrens. Conversations via phone and in person, 2019–2022.

Dunsmoor, Gary. Retired wildlife technician, Wisconsin DNR. Email communication, April 21, 2021. Phone and personal interviews, 2019–2022.

Evanson, Dave. President, Wisconsin Sharp-Tailed Grouse Society. Phone interview, March 31, 2020.

Finstad, Brian. Local historian, Gordon, Wisconsin. Phone interviews and email communications, 2020–2021.

Fitz, Tom. Geology professor, Northland College. Phone interviews, July 8, 2020, and April 29, 2021.

Garrett, Ben. Wildlife urban interface specialist, Wisconsin DNR. Phone interview, June 2, 2021.

Hanson, Bob. Wisconsin DNR wildlife biologist. Phone interview, May 15, 2020.

Heeringa, Brian. Wildlife biologist, US Forest Service. Phone interview, July 20, 2020.

Hillock, David. Great -great-grandson of Benjamin Hillock. Phone interview, May 9, 2022.

Hillock, Jeffrey. Descendant of Hillock family. Phone interview, June 11, 2018.

Hillock, Virgil, Sr. Grandson of Benjamin Hillock. Phone interview, July 17, 2018.

Hlina, Paul. Research botanist. Interviews, July 14, 31, 2020, and July 30, 2021. Namekagon Barrens Wildlife Area, Danbury, Wisconsin. Phone interview, July 14, 2020.

Holmes, Jason. Forester, Bayfield County Forestry and Parks. Phone interview, April 6, 2021.

Jensen, John. Frequent barrens visitor. Interview, June 4, 2020, Namekagon Barrens Wildlife Area, Danbury, Wisconsin.

Kell, Sherry. Great-granddaughter of Arvid Lyons. Phone interview, December 2, 2019.

Lambert, John M. Archaeologist, Illinois State Archaeological Society. Email communications, May 22, 2020, May 27, 2020, and April 7, 2021. Phone interview, April 5, 2021.

Leoso, Edith S. Tribal historic preservation officer, Bad River Band of Lake Superior Tribe of Chippewa. Phone and email communications, May–July 2021.

Luedeke, Mike. Former administrator, Burnett County Forests. Interviews and email communications, January 27, 2020, and April 6, 19, and 20, 2021.

Loebel, Thomas. Archaeologist, Illinois State Archaeological Survey. Email communication, April 14, 2020.

McAllister, Jerry. Veteran birdwatcher. Guided barrens bird walk, May 22, 2021. Email communications, September 16, 2020, and May 22, 2021.

Moss, Bruce. Former wildlife staff specialist, Wisconsin DNR. Phone interview, May 4, 2021.

Nichols, Jason. Administrator, Burnett County Forest and Parks administrator. Phone interview, April 19, 2021.

O'Connor, Ryan. Ecologist, Wisconsin DNR. Email communication, November 1, 2021.

Pfannkuche, Craig. Archivist, Chicago and Northwestern Historical Society. Email communications, July 19, 26, 27, and 28, 2018.

Riemer, Jim. Retired wildlife biologist, US Fish and Wildlife Service. Guided bog tour on Namekagen Barrens, June 12, 2021.

Roatch, Beatrice. Granddaughter of Samuel and LuAnn Turner. Phone interview, December 23, 2019.

Smith, Carol. Granddaughter of Ephraim Emery and Augusta Meeds. Interview, August 15, 2020, Gordon, Wisconsin.

Treuer, Anton. Professor of Ojibwe at Bemidji State University. Phone interviews, April 21, 2020, and April 12, 2021. Email communication, July 30, 2021.

Ullman, Dave. Geology professor, Northland College. Interview, October 25, 2019, Ashland, Wisconsin. Phone interview, March 23, 2022.

Van Denson, Jacqueline, Gail Marie Engstrom, and Sandra Van Denson. Descendants of Arvid Lyons. Email communication, March 23, 2020.

White, Dawn. Treaty Resource Specialist, Great Lakes Indian Fish & Wildlife Commission. Email communication, December 23, 2020.

Wiedenhoeft, Jane. Wolf expert, Wisconsin DNR. Email communication, July 8, 2020.

MEMOS AND CORRESPONDENCE

Hamerstrom, Frederick. Memo to J. B. Hale. May 25, 1966. Wisconsin Conservation Department. Provided by Nancy Christel, Wisconsin DNR office, Spooner, Wisconsin.

Dahlberg, B. L. Memo to J. R. Smith. July 17, 1864. Wisconsin Conservation Department. Provided by Nancy Christel, Wisconsin DNR office, Spooner.

Stone, Norman R. Memo to Emil Kaminski. November 28, 1955. Wisconsin Conservation Department. Provided by Nancy Christel, Wisconsin DNR office, Spooner.

Wisconsin Conservation Department internal memos from September 7, 1955, to May 17, 1967. Provided by Nancy Christel, Wisconsin DNR office, Spooner.

PRIMARY SOURCES

"1837 Land Cession Treaties with the Ojibwe and Dakota." Treaties Matter website. http://treatiesmatter.org/treaties/land/1837-ojibwe-dakota.

"1837 Treaty with the Chippewa, July 29, 1837." In *Indian Affairs: Laws and Treaties*. Vol. II, compiled and edited by Charles J. Kappler. Washington: Government Printing Office, 1904. GLIFWC website. https://glifwc.org/TreatyRights/TreatyChippewa07291837Web.pdf.

Arbuckle, Jerome. Narrative. Works Progress Administration, Chippewa Indian Historical Project Records, 1936–1942. Ashland Area Research Center, Ashland, Wisconsin.

Brunson, Alfred. Letter to Wisconsin Territorial Legislature. 1837. Wisconsin Digital Collections, University of Wisconsin.

Denomie, Florina. "Blueberry Picking among the Chippewas." Envelope 16, Works Progress Administration, Chippewa Indian Historical Project, 1936–1942. Ashland Area Research Center, Ashland, Wisconsin.

Henry, William A. *Northern Wisconsin: A Handbook for the Homeseeker*. Madison: Democrat Printing Company, State Printer, 1896.

Terry, Jennie Meeds. "Written Reminiscence of Life on the Barrens." Courtesy of her daughter, Carol Smith.

Zack, Mildred, and Dorothy Zach. "Written Reminiscence of Life on the Barrens." Burnett County Historical Society, Forts Folle Avoine, Danbury, Wisconsin.

REPORTS

Anderson, Derek, and Paul Hlina. Report on the Barrens Flora of the Northwest Sands Region of Wisconsin. Superior, WI: Self-published, 2022.

Bayfield County Forest Barrens Management Plan. 2020–2035. Bayfield County Forestry Department, Bayfield, Wisconsin. https://wi-bayfield county.civicplus.com/DocumentCenter/View/10246/Barnes-Barrens -Management-Plan---20200510-Final-Draft-1?bidId=.

Bayfield County Forest Comprehensive Land Use Plan, 2021–2035. Barnes Barrens Management Plan. www.bayfieldcounty.wi.gov/DocumentCenter /View/11733/Bayfield-County-2021-2035-Comp-Plan?bidId=.

Board of Commissioners of Public Lands. "Wisconsin Public Land Survey Records: Original Field Notes and Plat Maps." Wisconsin Digital Collections, University of Wisconsin. https://digicoll.library.wisc.edu/SurveyNotes /SurveyNotesHome.html.

Fandel, Sharon, and Scott Hull. "Wisconsin Sharp-Tailed Grouse: A Comprehensive Management and Conservation Strategy." Wisconsin DNR. May 2011. https://p.widencdn.net/aqkuex/stgrplan.

Fellows, Hiram C. "Field Notes for Township 42 North Range 14 West." Internal Survey, General Description. Wisconsin Public Land Survey Records, Board of Commissioners of Public Lands. Wisconsin Digital Collections. https://digicoll.library.wisc.edu/SurveyNotes/SurveyNotesHome.html.

Haywood, Norman. "A Phase II Archaeological Evaluation of the Bowling Lane Site, A Multicomponent Site in Gordon, Douglas County, Wisconsin." Commissioned by the Wisconsin Department of Transportation. December 1991.

US Forest Service. Moquah Barrens Management Plan. 2009. www.fs
.usda.gov/detail/cnnf/landmanagement/resourcemanagement/?cid=
fseprd577751.

Wisconsin Aerial Photography Collection. State Cartographer's Office,
University of Wisconsin–Madison. www.sco.wisc.edu/maps/aerial
-photography/.

Wisconsin Department of Natural Resources. Northwest Sands Regional Master Plan. February 2019. https://embed.widencdn.net/pdf/plus/widnr/
04cfzb02a5/NorthwestSandsRegionalMasterPlan_WholePlan.pdf.

Wisconsin Prairie Grouse Management Policy. Wisconsin Conservation Commission. May 14, 1953. Provided by Nancy Christel, Wisconsin DNR office,
Spooner.

Wisconsin Initiative on Climate Change Impacts. *Wisconsin's Changing Climate: Impacts and Adaptation.* 2011. Nelson Institute for Environmental
Studies and Wisconsin Department of Natural Resources. https://wicci
.wisc.edu/2011-assessment-report/.

Wisconsin Land Inventory Land Cover Map. Town of Blaine, Burnett County.
Land Economic Inventory Maps Collection (Bordner Survey). University
of Wisconsin–Madison Digital Collections. https://search.library.wisc
.edu/digital/ANOKUGSGWNFIGV9C/full/AJPAJ3GEKGEKV58D.

INDEX

Note: Page numbers in *italic type* refer to illustrations.

About the Author

ANTONIO RODRIGUEZ

Dave Peters spent more than forty years as a journalist, including work as a reporter and editor for the *St. Paul Pioneer Press*, the *Minneapolis Star Tribune*, and Minnesota Public Radio. He and his wife, Lisa, live in St. Paul, Minnesota, and spend much of their time at a cabin in the Northwest Sands of Wisconsin, near Danbury. He is a member of the Friends of the Namekagon Barrens Wildlife Area.